Thomas Tod Stoddart, Anna M. Stoddart

Angling Songs

Thomas Tod Stoddart, Anna M. Stoddart

Angling Songs

ISBN/EAN: 9783337007270

Printed in Europe, USA, Canada, Australia, Japan

Cover: Foto ©Thomas Meinert / pixelio.de

More available books at **www.hansebooks.com**

ANGLING SONGS

BY

THOMAS TOD STODDART

With a Memoir

BY

ANNA M. STODDART

WILLIAM BLACKWOOD AND SONS
EDINBURGH AND LONDON
MDCCCLXXXIX

Thomas T Stoddart

To

Sir GEORGE DOUGLAS, *Bart., of Springwood Park, Kelso; and to My Father's Old Friends,* JAMES TAIT, *Esq., of Langrigg;* JAMES ELLIOT, *Esq., Galalaw; and* ROBERT FRAIN, *Esq., as well as to those of his Brother Anglers of Tweed and Teviot who survive him, and hold him in kindly remembrance,*

THIS MEMOIR IS DEDICATED BY

ANNA M. STODDART.

CONTENTS.

	PAGE
MEMOIR	1
ELEGY	194

ANGLING SONGS—

THE ANGLER'S VINDICATION	201
TROLLING SONG	204
THE ANGLER'S COMPLAINT	206
TO THE NAIRN	208
SONG	210
THE HOLY-WELL POOL	212
MUSINGS	215
SONNET—CONAN FALLS	217
THE TAKING OF THE SALMON	218
SEEK YE WHAR THE BURNIE TRAVELS	222
THE VOICE OF THE CUCKOO	224
O WAKEN, WINDS, WAKEN!	226
SONNET—THE ETTRICK SHEPHERD	228
THE RIVER	229
TROLLING SONG	231
THE SEA-TROUT GREY	233
AN ANGLER'S RAMBLES	235
DRINKING SONG	238

CONTENTS.

ANGLING SONGS—

	PAGE
THE YELLOW FINS O' YARROW	240
A PICTURE	242
A PECK O' TROUBLES	243
THE ANGLER'S BENEDICTION	246
SONNET—THE RIVER EDEN	248
WHEN THE STREAMS RISE	249
BRING THE ROD, THE LINE, THE REEL!	252
THE FLEE	254
THE ANGLER'S TRYSTING-TREE	255
THE LAIRD'S CAST	257
SONNET	260
THE GENTLE CRAFT	261
YE WARDERS OF THE WATERS	263
THE ANGLER'S JOYS	265
THE BONNIE TWEED	268
THE BREEZE IS ON	271
THE ANGLER'S INVITATION	274
I SIT BY THE RIVER	275
THE ANGLER'S CHOICE	277
TO THE TWEED	280
THE PIKE	284
SONNET	287
THE HAPPY ANGLER	288
SONNET	290
THE STREAMS OF OLD SCOTLAND	291
MY AIN WEE FISHER BOY	293
GOOD CHEER! BROTHER ANGLER	294
A LOCH SCENE	296
OWER AT THE CAULD-FOOT	300

CONTENTS.

ANGLING SONGS—

	PAGE
THE ANGLER'S GRAVE	304
DRINKING SONG	306
THE FAIRY ANGLER	308
FAIRY'S SONG	310
ANGLING ON A SUMMER NIGHT	311
WE PART NOT THUS	314
THE BURNING OF THE WATER	316
THE LYNNS OF GLENDEVON	319
SONNET—THE FINDHORN	321
FISHER WATTY	322

MEMOIR.

My father called one day on Henry Glassford Bell, and the genial Sheriff hailed him with the very natural question, "Well, Tom, and what are you doing now?" With a moment's resentment, my father brought his friend to his bearings. "Doing? Man, I'm an angler."

That answer sounded the keynote of his life, and suggested at once its ambitions and their realisation. His wishes, his tastes, his skill, his character all helped to make him what he was—an angler; and the bias that found support in these presided over his lot, and led him to choose for its conditions just those which were most in its favour. His happiness was to be near the two beloved streams of Tweed and Teviot; his glory was to know them in every mood, to be familiar with their every current and eddy and tributary, their sleepy willow-shaded pools and glancing silvery reaches, their still waters and noisy caulds, their swift red spates and stagnant shallows, the birds that haunted their banks, the very sedges and forget-me-nots that fringed their margins. However far afield he went—and at one time and another he fished almost every river, loch, and burn in Scotland—he came back to his Tweedside home with boundless content. The Tweed was the best of rivers to his thinking, and next best was the Teviot, and he did not care to stay long away from them. Only one other river-valley vied in his regard with theirs—the Vale of Yarrow and its lochs.

Besides these, other streams had their qualities, could be fished for passing pleasure, could be critically discussed and catalogued in his diary, could furnish adventures, and even give good sport; but their waters had no music in their murmur, no thrill of countless recollections in their rush.

As his best hours were passed in their neighbourhood, he seldom left it; so that his life is that of a man who stayed chiefly at home, and found all needful variety in the gentle and unexciting changes which brighten home and country life.

Along with his devotion to angling, there is most worthy of note his gift of unwearied friendship. The men who won his regard in his youth retained it while they lived; and when they died, they took away with them the sources of much of his constant happiness, leaving behind them memories on which he touched from time to time with tender reverence. He had the great endowment of a heart to warm and freshen every stage of his life; and if at times it invited and accentuated its griefs and losses, still it did not fail him even in these, but helped him to store up their wreckage, and to mantle it with associations.

The poems which follow this short Memoir

reveal him in both these characters. The circumstances which I have now to relate only confirm the self-revelation of his childlike, single-minded, impulsive, loyal and gifted nature.

Early in this century a number of documents relating to the Stoddart family were left in the charge of an eccentric old lady, a Miss Helen Stoddart, who lived in Leith. It occurred to her that she was bewitched, and that the evil influence came from the seals and decorated initials of the family papers. She cut some of these off and burned them; but finding herself no better, and still suspecting the papers, she tossed a number of them wholesale into the fire. The oldest looked most dangerous, and were therefore first sacrificed, and many of those she spared were torn and defaced. The few remaining papers give data of the family during the seventeenth and eighteenth centuries. Beyond the year 1600 we have to trust to oral traditions and to the information of a well-known Border antiquarian, the late Mr. Scott of Raeburn. These tell us that the old name was Stoutheart; that in the fourteenth and fifteenth centuries the Stouthearts were well known in both Liddesdale and Ettrick; that a Stoutheart was laird of Comiston in Liddesdale, and another was laird of Kershope in Northumberland; while the churchyard which overhangs St. Mary's Loch bore evidence half a century ago to the existence of Stouthearts in Ettrick in 1462. The lettering on this ancient tombstone is no longer legible. They were Border people, excitable and litigious, but bearing a high character for honesty in rough and treacherous times, when self-interest was the rule of conduct, and lawless aggression its manifestation. Mr. Scott's researches in Border history led him to the conclusion that at a time when lands changed their lords for many a reason,—confiscation, violence, treachery, favouritism,—the Stouthearts held theirs by the honest right of purchase, a right not so picturesque, perhaps, but certainly more creditable. There is documentary evidence that in 1508 the lands of

Baillielees and Clowburn, in the Forest of Ettrick, belonged to a branch of the family, as they were sold by the owners to Gilbert Elliot of Stobbs in that year. In 1605, two brothers, John and William Stoddart, descendants of the laird of Baillielees, bought the property of Williamhope in Peeblesshire. This land lies on the slope of the watershed between Tweed and Yarrow, and inclines chiefly toward the former. Glenkinnon is at its foot, the streamlet making for the Tweed. The glen gives it the Border term of "hope;" and it is just possible, as Mr. Craig Brown suggests, that to the death of William, Earl of Douglas, in 1303, close to the spot, it owes the rest of its name. Williamhope belonged to Thomas Ker of Mersington, by a grant from Queen Mary, and the Stoddarts bought the land from the Kers. The immediate descendants of the first Stoddarts of Williamhope were strong Covenanters. They added by their own personal sufferings in the cause, and by the protection they gave to persecuted Covenanters, to the volume of heroic endurance and effort made by the Borderers at that time. One laird of Williamhope was seized after the Battle of Drumclog, held captive first by one person, and then by another, his captors making futile efforts to force him to forswear the cause, until, wearying of his obstinacy, they took his money instead of his oath, and he was set at liberty on payment of five hundred merks. His brother was hunted amongst the hills, and died of exposure and starvation. There used to be a large artificial cave in the steep bank of Glenkinnon Burn, a short distance from the house, lined with solid masonry and sixteen feet square, its entrance small and sheltered by the overhanging bank. Here many a fugitive was secured from the soldiery, and easily supplied with food from the house. The laird was suspected, and he and his brothers were fined in 1679 for harbouring Covenanters. This laird had other claims to notice besides his stubborn Presbyterianism. His name was John Stoddart, and, as well as his own property of Williamhope, he and his brothers farmed Tinnis and Lewinshope on the Philiphaugh estate. He seems to have lived as much at these farms as at Williamhope, and this connection between the Murrays and the Stoddarts led to a neighbourly friendship which lasted for some generations.

John Stoddart was a man of marked individuality, both of character and person. A tall man, of immense strength, he excelled all the Selkirkshire men of his day in athletic feats, and was in high repute for running, wrestling, and carrying weights. His arms were of unusual length and very strong, so that he could lift a stone which tasked five ordinary men at once. This feat won him the nicknames of the "Beetle of Yarrow" and "Long-arms;" and fifty years ago the memory of his strength still lingered in Yarrow, and the stone in question lay in the manse-garden. He had received a legal education, and was a man of much natural ability, so that Murray of Philiphaugh, who was hereditary

Sheriff of Selkirkshire, secured for him the appointment of Sheriff-Depute, and in 1690 he was made Commissioner of Supply to the Scottish Parliament for the town of Lanark. He married early in life, but his wife died, leaving one daughter. For many years he remained a widower, living chiefly at Tinnis with his daughter. Here in 1695 he had a serious illness, and his next of kin arrived in full expectation of his immediate death. His daughter was with him, and in a room close to the sick-room the expectant heirs were assembled. Absorbed in the exciting prospect of inheritance, they began to quarrel over the division of his property, and their voices, raised in unseemly wrath, reached the Sheriff's ears. He got up, and, gaunt and white as he was, clad in his nightshirt, he opened the door of the room in which they were disputing, and lifting his long and bony arm, bade them begone, for they were no heirs of his. They fled from the house, followed by the parting threat that he would marry that very year and thwart their greed. And so he did, by sheer force of will shaking off a malady that seemed mortal, and marrying the widow of Mr. Dalgleish of Fastheugh. This lady's maiden name was Martha Muir, and she was the daughter of Lieutenant-Colonel John Muir of Anniston in Clydesdale, descended from Rowallan, the father of Elizabeth More, who was Robert the Second's wife. She had two sons when she married the Sheriff, and they lived at Tinnis afterwards, and were great favourites with their stepfather. But he prepared a complete outfit for his bride, and would not allow her to wear anything which had the least association with her former husband, all such belongings being packed up and returned to Fastheugh. His threat to his kinsmen proved valid, for he lived long enough to become the father of two sons, John and Thomas, and died in June 1699, three years after his second marriage. His widow married a third time, three years after his death, a son of Mr. Curror of Hartwoodburn, and Dalgleishes, Stoddarts, and Currors lived in amity all together.

The Sheriff's elder son, John, was well educated, and joined Lord Jedburgh's regiment in 1715, his commission of captain being signed by the Duke of Buccleugh. In 1718, when he came of age, he bought the property of Hartwoodburn from the Currors, and made the house on it his chief residence. In 1720 he married Helen Veitch, daughter of Mr. Veitch of the Glen, the well-known Covenanter. They had a large family, but most of the children died young, and the unhealthy situation of Hartwoodburn was blamed for this mortality. John Stoddart tired of the place, and sold it in 1757 to Mr. Pringle. After this he lived at Williamhope and Canobie, and died at the latter place in 1770, he and his wife being both buried in Yarrow churchyard, in the same grave as his father, the Sheriff-Depute. His fifth son, Thomas, succeeded to Williamhope, the others having died in childhood. Thomas Stoddart was at the time of his father's death a middle-aged man, married, and resident in Leith, where he had entered into partnership with his father-in-law, Mr. Tod, a Baltic timber-merchant. He sold Williamhope as soon as he came into possession to Mr. Gilbert Innes of Stow, and the " Summer Hill" above Glenkinnon Burn is now the property of Lady Reay. Mr. Thomas Stoddart made his home in Leith, and brought up there a family of seven sons and five daughters. Although he had severed his connection with Yarrow and Williamhope, his youth at Hartwoodburn had left its mark in a strong attachment to his native hills and glens. He had learned the joys of angling in his boyhood, and knew the secrets of every stream in Yarrow and Ettrick, and year after year, while he was able, he returned to them to fish. The old friendship between Murrays and Stoddarts lasted during his lifetime, and his genial nature and pleasant looks made him a favourite at the Hangingshaw, where he often stayed, and where he was a guest when the house was destroyed by fire, following which disaster that part of Philiphaugh passed into the hands of Mr. Johnstone of Alva. Indeed, he was better fitted by character and tastes for the life of a country gentleman than for that of a man of business, a certain ingenuousness and simplicity of nature laying him open to the sharp practice which even then invaded the province of commerce, and by which he was worsted in the struggle for wealth. He lived to a great age, dying in 1816 in his eighty-second year, provided for during the last years of his life by his sons. Of these, two held commissions in the army, and three entered the navy. It is with one of these last that my story has to do. He was the third son, Pringle Stoddart, and was born on 23rd May 1768. As a boy, he went to Catterick in Yorkshire to school, and at the age of fourteen was sent to Madras in an East-Indiaman commanded by Captain Tod. The vessel in which he sailed was detained at the Mother Bank, and while there he saw the sinking of the *Royal George* with eight hundred persons on board, all drowned. The voyage to Madras took seven months, and the East-Indiamen sailed as far as Gibraltar with the grand fleet under the command of Lord Howe, bound for the relief of that place. When Captain Tod reached Madras, he strongly recommended his young midshipman to enter the Royal Navy, in which men and officers were much needed at the time. Pringle Stoddart and a messmate followed his advice and entered the *Exeter* as midshipmen. This vessel was one of the fleet under Sir Edward Hughes lying in the roads at Madras. The boy soon began his long experience of active service, for, in the month in which he joined, the fleet sailed to meet the French ships under De Suffrein, and his young comrade was shot in the encounter which followed off Cuddalore. His whole career in the navy was one of unremitting activity. The times were stirring ones for our fleet, and it fell to his share to take part in no fewer than thirteen naval engagements. Our chief foes were the French; and between the years 1793 and 1807 he was present, under different commanders, at encounters with their fleets in many different parts of the world. Perhaps the most important of his services were those rendered in Egypt in 1801, while in the *Kent.* He was mentioned with high praise by both Sir Ralph Abercromby and Sir Sidney Smith. He took part also in the siege of Copenhagen, and Admiral Gambier complimented him on the bravery and energy with which he fought in a prolonged contest with a Danish flotilla. How much he did, however, was never known, as these facts are gleaned from the very scanty record he kept of his services, and the stern silence he maintained on all matters relating to them was never broken even to his sons, who would gladly have listened to some account of his adventures. This silence told against his interests. He belonged to a bygone generation, which counted services and sufferings for the country as duties, not as merits to be used, with loud reiteration, as purchase-price for promotion and honours. And so this silent hero, with many others of his time, was not greatly recompensed; and when he died, at the age of eighty, held only the brevet rank of Rear-Admiral. Some incidents of his career filtered out after his death. One of the most interesting of these was, that while second in command of a ship at the Texel, where the fleet lay at anchor, ready to transport our troops so soon as the weather was favourable to the dangerous passage, he tired of the inaction, during which the men were sickening of dysentery, and locking his tipsy commander into his cabin, lightened his ship for the passage, set sail for England, disembarked his troops, and returned to his station at the Texel ready for a new cargo. This smart action came under the head of insubordination, so their Lordships administered reproof with one hand and promotion with the other.

In 1807 Captain Pringle Stoddart married Miss Frances Sprot, a daughter of Mr. James Sprot of Edinburgh. The acquaintance was made in London, where Miss Sprot kept house in Nightingale Lane, Clapham, for her brother John, who realised a large fortune in business.

The newly-married couple made their home in Edinburgh, and in Argyle Square, on the 14th of February 1810, my father was born. Their first child was a daughter, called Frances after her mother, but my father was their eldest son; and the names Thomas Tod, which were given him, combined a compliment to both his grandparents, who were living in Leith. The house in Argyle Square had been Principal Robertson's, and in it he had written his Histories of Charles V. and of America. The New Town of Edinburgh was of limited extent in those days, and its West End had hardly made a beginning. As that extended, the squares and streets of the Old Town, in spite of all their associations with the historic and social past of Edinburgh, fell into disrepute, and there was much migration of the respectable across the valley into the handsome stone houses ranged in imposing lines on the north side. The old houses fell lower in the scale of occupants, and as new needs developed, many of them were swept away. Argyle Square

B

was a sacrifice of this sort, and very suitably gave place, when its time came, to the buildings of the Industrial Museum. Captain Stoddart's first migration was to Abercromby Place, where several of his succeeding children were born; but feeling the want of out-of-door space for the growing family, he removed after a few years to Kirkbraehead, a house at that time considered to be in the country, and standing on what is now Rutland Square. Here there was a large and delightful garden, containing many attractions, not the least of which was a pond in which perch might be caught. Captain Stoddart was fond of gardening, and shared the prevailing taste for Dutch bulbs. A little girl who came to play in the garden knocked the head off a favourite tulip, and for this Tom got the blame and took a vicarious thrashing without a word. Thrashings were a familiar feature in his upbringing and that of his brothers. Their father, a stern disciplinarian on board ship, was no less so at home. His own career had been one of duty and endurance, and he did his best to bring the experience of his sons up to the same level. The parental severity was sometimes overstrained, and Tom, with a nature all unlike his father's, got from very early years more than his due share of thrashings. These would scarcely predispose him to take just the same view of duty as did his father, and the divergence of opinion took expression early.

The nursery circle increased and was completed during the years spent at Kirkbrachead, four sons and three daughters making up its sum; and when the land covered by their pleasant home was wanted for the houses of Rutland Square, the family removed first to Albany Street, and then finally, in 1826, to No. 10 Bellevue Crescent. This remained the centre for many subsequent years, and the home-house to which married sons and daughters, and the wanderers which events made of two sons of the house, returned as guests in the years to come.

My father must have been about nine years

old when the family removed from Kirkbraehead to Albany Street, and his education had begun. His first teachers, men of the old school, who believed in the tawse, grounded him well in Latin and English subjects; but they held short sway, as, when he reached the age of ten, he and one of his brothers were sent to a Moravian school at Fairfield in Lancashire. His recollections of this school were far from pleasant, and he made scant progress during his stay. No doubt the ushers on their part found him somewhat intractable; for while too young to be greatly concerned at the classic sufferings of Dido and the invectives of Cicero, his imagination had roused to themes of its own choice, and its ambitious stirrings absorbed all the attention which should have gone to drudgery at the Latin Grammar. At the age of ten, his whole desire was to produce an immortal tragedy. To inspire his mind with plot and material, he saved his pocket-money to buy a kind of literature known then and now as "penny dreadfuls!" the taste for which revives from time to time, and seems to be deeply rooted in human nature. These sheets were illustrated with the ghastly details of many a murder, shipwreck, feat of brigandage, highway robbery, and suicide, and formed just such a library of horrors as would excite the impressionable fancy of the budding poet. He does not seem to have believed the tales he read, and over which he gloated; nor was he frightened by them, as many a boy of his age would have been. He reckoned them, with practical philosophy, as so much material, and proceeded to construct his tragedies on the basis of plots which they suggested. Every other dramatic form he despised. Blood and battle were the powers with which he worked, and with no meaner tools. At these tragedies he laboured in lesson-time and out of it, much to his disadvantage with the authorities, and doubtless not greatly to his advantage otherwise. Not one of them remains to contrast with the work of his later life. The mood lasted in milder form during a decade of years, and, as we shall see, exhausted itself in the "Deathwake" and "Abel Massinger."

The little dramatist emerged from his labours at the call of patriotism, however, and fought a fierce battle with a Manchester boy who had dared to sneer at Scotland and its natives; but unhappily he was beaten, and had besides to suffer the indignity of a caning from the German usher for fighting. From Fairfield he soon went home, and was then sent to the Edinburgh High School, where some years of systematic training fitted him for the University of Edinburgh, on whose student-roll he was entered in 1825, at the age of fifteen.

But the years between Fairfield and the University brought other gain besides that of study. Captain Stoddart had gathered from his father both zeal for angling and its art, although the latter was confined in those days to bait-fishing. In the preceding century the Water of Leith had been a prime trouting-stream, to which salmon were still attracted; and it is difficult for those who now see its handful of perturbed water at the mercy of a group of mills to realise that in the past it was deemed worthy of royal protection, and was preserved as a salmon-river by Act of Parliament. In 1780, my grandfather, then a boy twelve years old, had assisted in catching a salmon out of it. His love of fishing lasted all his life, and his four sons soon became his eager followers. They did his teaching credit, for all were enthusiastic and skilful anglers, although only in my father's case did the passion become the master of his destiny. The first lesson he got was in some holiday-time before he went to Fairfield, and when the family was in summer-bathing quarters in Elie. Near that town a tiny streamlet falls into the Firth of Forth, known as the Cockle Mill Burn, and out of it he pulled triumphantly his first trout, about half a pound in weight. Many successes followed, trouts, eels, and flounders, and the youngster's fate was fixed. Stern Tragedy might woo him when away from rippling brooks and dimpling lochs, but with the spring and the mayfly, the dagger dipped in gore paled before the supple rod and the dainty midge; for the finer art of fly-fishing soon attracted him, and led him to seek other teachers than those of the older school. The best of these was an old man of the kind to whom boys are inevitably attracted, in the absence of gamekeepers, and the sociable, knowing, casual sportsmen that idle about country places. His name was Bill Dawson, and he kept a little tackle-shop in the High Street of Edinburgh, in an upper flat of one of its lofty houses. Up the stairs the boys gladly toiled for their lines and hooks, knowing that a valuable gossip with the lame old man would be thrown into the bargain. He was an excellent fly-fisher, and made his own lures, tiny midges dressed with a few threads of fur and feather. He knew every cast in the Water of Leith, and drew out of it many a dish of trout on summer afternoons, always with the fly; and he taught his little customer every trick and turn of the rod he knew. But it was farther afield that the boy caught his first prize with the fly, and not in Dawson's company. A summer holiday at Callander led him to the Teith to make trial of his new knowledge, and here, near the Camp, with a brown hackle, he pulled out a parr as his first success in fly-fishing. Not a burn nor loch near Callander was left untried, and in one of the latter he caught his first pike; a mighty fish he thought it, for it weighed three pounds. He had tried and proved his rudimentary knowledge, and so laid the foundation for all the variations and developments of the art which he afterwards practised and described so well.

The campaigns with France had brought amongst us as prisoners of war many officers of the French army. One of these, well known in Edinburgh during the first part of this century, had elected to make his home there. This was M. Senebier, and amongst the many claims he had to popularity, his skill as a fisher counted chief with boys. He was adventurous too in the use of bait, and his receipt for potting salmon-roe remained one of the treasured spoils of my father's acquaintance with him. All influences, hereditary and of circumstance, were strengthening the inborn taste; and although the Tragic Muse still dallied with his fancy, interests were preparing which should finally overcome her attractions, and leave him undisturbed to give his imagination, as well as his mind and his leisure, to the art and literature of angling.

Midsummer holidays in the country, Saturday holidays by the Water of Leith, these last sometimes yielding six and seven dozen dainty fullfed trout, cherished the passion and ripened his skill. There were other haunts of the trout near Edinburgh with which he and his brothers grew familiar—the Almond, the Gogar Burn, the two Esks, and the Compensation Pond. This last was a favourite resort, the walk to and from the Pentland Hills adding enjoyment to the excursion. Often the boys started early on Saturday morning, and came home late at night. Very late hours were strictly forbidden, as next day was Sunday; and it is on record that one evening, being somewhat belated, and finding an empty and driverless hearse standing at a toll-door, the horses' heads turned towards Edinburgh, they got inside before the tipsy driver came out, and sat in solemn silence till he had driven a short distance, when his ears were assailed with unearthly howls and shrieks and songs from the hearse, so that in mortal terror he lashed the horses into a gallop, and they rattled along at a most unholy pace. A steep ascent near Edinburgh forced the unhappy man to slacken speed, and the boys, relapsing into silence, slid out one after the other, much refreshed by the rest, and helped on their way by the funereal lift. Four good boys arrived at home in proper time, and without a hint on their ingenuous faces of how they had fared thither.

The winter holidays were devoted to rhyming. Between his thirteenth and his sixteenth years he fashioned a store of verses, fluent and imitative of necessity—Campbell and Byron the masters of his imagination and the models of his style. He tried them in all their variations, Byron being distinctly the more influential of the two. Spirits, wizards, knights, royalties, nuns, pirates, and "strangers" figure in these effusions, but here and there is a touch of that love of Nature which grew into a characteristic of his ripened powers. At the age of fourteen he wore a rathe willow for some flouting Phyllida, probably a pupil at the boarding-school next door, and filled pages with the rhyme of his love and scorn.

In 1825 my father began his attendance at college classes. A career at the Scottish Bar was planned for him; for it is the fate of poetic youths to be bred to the law. But indeed no profession would have suited a temperament which shrank as his did from the details and responsibilities of practical business, though it seemed very natural at the time to suppose that a lad with a turn for reading and some gift of eloquence would cut a figure at the Bar. His curriculum at the University included at first the usual classes, and the class-tickets which he preserved are many of them endorsed with the Professors' approbation, notably that bearing Professor John Wilson's signature. For it was here that he first came in contact with that brilliant figure which dominated the generation of men of letters following Sir Walter Scott. Young as he was, my father felt his fascination, sat spell-bound under an eloquence which owed much of its power to impressive gesture and the free grandeur of his face and form; and worked with all his heart in Moral Philosophy, the great Professor's subject. Here, too, he met classmates destined to become friends and companions for many a year. William Aytoun and John Wilson, the Professor's son, were, in respect of the bearing they had on his own life and development, the most significant friends he made at this time. Their friendship and his student zeal won him many an invitation to the Professor's house, and by degrees he grew into the habit of intimacy there, and was a familiar form in its home circle. The intimacy was a source of much stimulus to him on every but the practical side; for if material advancement be the main thing needful, it was perhaps to some extent injurious. In those young days, with a whole world of experiences before him, the unquestioned security of an affluent home at his back, the sense of growing powers and the widening horizon of contact with men of genius, the future seemed easy and promising—a tournament where the victorious knights wore the visor of genius and slew with the shaft of wit. The hours spent in the Professor's house grew to yield him the keenest pleasure of his life, and the encouragement and appreciation which his dreams and desires excited there fostered more and more the individuality which already strongly marked his nature, and which other considerations failed to check. Individuality was at a premium in that house, and the likeness of its intimates chiefly consisted in admiring and displaying each other's unlikeness. Not that they spared each other's weaknesses; the free encounter of jeers and gibes ran high, but always tempered by the condition of wit; and so the brilliant battles ended ever in amity. Men, not manners, were cultivated there, and yet so cultivated that manners were not wanting. The atmosphere of such a house was of necessity a contrast to the well-ordered, conventional home from which thrilling interests were sternly excluded as scarcely reputable, and where obedience and self-repression were the cardinal virtues of youth. The friends of the home were men like their host, the very thews and sinews of the country in her times of peril, heroes to others of the boys, but to Tom inexpressibly uninteresting. The friends of the house where he loved to spend his leisure were Aytoun, Ferrier, and Gordon, De Quincey, Hartley Coleridge and the Ettrick Shepherd, "Delta" and Henry Glassford Bell—to him the very salt of the earth. It cannot be gainsaid that much might be urged on either side—that the strain was inevitable. Unfortunately, the father and son discussed the difference too often and too obstinately, with too little sympathy on either side. The boy continued to seek the converse and association which answered his nature and roused his capacities, diverting them more and more from the restricted channels which led to worldly success, and firing them with large aims and impulses, glowing with promise of heroic reward, but not calculated to yield a yearly income.

For the rest, these days of intimacy with the Wilsons heaped up for him a store of lifelong recollections; and in recalling them, one seems again to touch the "vanished hand" of that brilliant generation whose influence has passed away. At the Professor's table, vivacious, sparkling, original conversation was the rule; guests unable to contribute to it seldom sat there; sons, daughters, and habitués came primed with fresh and witty comment and story. Eccentricity, recklessness, the freest discussion were permitted; but all must be with flow of fancy, thought, and racy expression. Only John Wilson himself, or his frequent visitor, De Quincey, was allowed at times to dominate the talk; and my father used to say that when these rare monopolies took place, the rest sat entranced, hanging on the lips of the speaker. De Quincey he often met, an old-looking man more than sixty years ago. One day when he was talking to the Professor in the library, De Quincey came in dressed only in a nightshirt, with his arms full of books. He took no notice of them, but returned the books to the shelves, collected another armful, and left the room. He would lie in bed for days, till he had read all the new books his host possessed, and then he would get up, dress, and behave much as other people. The Wilsons were endlessly kind and forbearing to him, supplying his wants, giving him money, which as often as not he tossed to the first beggar he met, keeping him in their house for weeks and months in spite of every provoking habit, admiring and delighting in him when he joined their meals, and opened out into a flow of fascinating talk, made electrifying sometimes by his power of subtle argument. The Professor had his times of abstraction from the talk of the supper-table. When his article for *Blackwood* was due, and the printer's devil sat cooling his heels in the hall, he would appear in his accustomed place, but without his accustomed mien, coatless, silent, ominous, with vacant eye, withdrawn in spirit from the bright talk and laughter, which were no whit intermitted, and after eating what he wished, would rise and leave the table without a word, to return an hour or so after, clothed and in his usual mind, a free and happy man, disemburdened for the nonce. No one spoke to him on those occasions, and no one minded him.

The more important friendships which grew out of this intercourse were one with John Wilson, the Professor's son, which lasted his lifetime, and one with William Aytoun, afterwards the Professor's son-in-law, which was of great interest and importance to my father for some ten years or more, but which did not persevere much further. The three lads fell into the habit of making holiday excursions together. They were about the same age, and had the same tastes, amongst these that of fishing. A hereditary tie existed between my father and the hills and streams of Yarrow. Chance and some other circumstances were beginning to call into play the strong attraction of the place. The friends went together, accompanied, I believe, by Professor Wilson, to Innerleithen, to see the St. Ronan's Games in 1826. James Hogg, the Ettrick Shepherd, was there, and my father made his acquaintance. The mixture of simplicity, shrewdness, and genius which distinguished Hogg attracted him greatly, and resulted in a friendship which lasted till Hogg's death. This circumstance alone would have led my father's steps to Yarrow; but his interest in the district was much stimulated by the visits paid to it about the same time by my grandfather.

Captain Stoddart had secured from his father as many verbal details of his ancestry as the old gentleman could recollect, and had committed them to writing. He was anxious to supplement them by what information he could glean from the neighbourhood of their old possessions, and to that end opened correspondence with several likely authorities. One of these was Dr. Russell, minister of Yarrow, and from him he learned that the tomb of the Sheriff and his son was in disrepair. He paid the Yarrow churchyard several visits, and his eldest son went with him on at least one occasion, and caught the infection of interest in his Border ancestry. Captain Stoddart made a careful examination of the churchyards of Yarrow, and restored the headstones and tabular memorial stones which proved to belong to the graves of his forefathers. His quest made some sensation in the quiet valley, and was talked of about a generation later as one of the notable events of the past. Neglect is so surely the portion of the dead, that the spectacle of this tall, stern man searching forgotten graves, and rescuing from oblivion names already effaced and memories that had ceased to be remembered, startled and excited the country-folk as an apparition might have done or a miracle. From some members of his own house he got scant sympathy, and a witty cartoon made its appearance in the family, in which he sat grim and silent on a low churchyard wall, rod in hand, fishing in the moonlight in a sea of ruined graves overgrown with nettles, and below the legend ran :—

> "His rod was made of the family tree,
> His line was a long line of ancestry;
> He baited his hook with dead men's marrow,
> And he sat and he bobbed for the Beetle of Yarrow.
> He bobbed till the moon rose over the hill,
> And, for aught that I know, he is sitting there still,
> Though the wind may blow and the nettles may wave,
> And never a rise can he get from the grave."

The final restorations were made in 1828, and in the same year William Aytoun, young John Wilson, and my father made their first appearance at St. Mary's Loch and the little cottage belonging to Tibbie Shiels, which was from that time to become so famous. They had another companion, who, I fancy, must have been either Archibald Campbell Swinton or a medical student called Leitch. Mrs. Richardson was then scarcely fifty years old, a shrewd, kindly, comely woman, tenanting the cottage on the strip of land between St. Mary's Loch and the Loch of the Lowes. She had succeeded to the tenancy on the death of her husband, a Dalesman from Westmoreland who had come to Ettrick in Lord Napier's service, and marrying Isabella Shiels, had settled in the little cottage, living long enough to become the father of three sons and three daughters. The youngest of these was about ten years old in 1828, and is now the grey-haired tenant of St. Mary's Cottage, keeping up its hospitable renown. But then he was "just a callant," as he says himself, although old enough to notice the first arrival of the four lads whose coming heralded a season of glory for the place. Mrs. Richardson was by that time a widow, and had reverted in Border fashion to her maiden name in its familiar form of Tibbie Shiels. She had permission to make the cottage a kind of primitive inn, on condition that she sold neither wine nor spirits. And here the four young anglers, who had walked over the hills and through Traquair from Innerleithen, the scene of the St. Ronan's Games, found some eccentric worthies, regular guests at the cottage, already installed. Tibbie made room for the newcomers, however, provided as they were with a recommendation from her friend and neighbour James Hogg; and here, in the little home sheltered by a rich growth of rowans, hawthorns, laburnums, firs, and sycamores, they lived from the 10th of July to the end of the month, delighting in the beauty and unrestraint of the place, and winning by their delight the freedom of the whole neighbourhood. Their quarters were cramped enough, and all four slept in a tiny attic with two press-beds, and ate their own trout, supplemented by rashers of bacon and mutton-chops, by the best of scones and butter and milk; but their withdrawing-rooms were the borders of the lochs and the sides of the grassy hills. The power of Yarrow took them captive, and held them in willing bondage all the years of their lives. Tibbie's heart warmed to them for their enjoyment, and, speaking of them in after years, she said, "Eh! but they were ra'al happy." They were contented in those early days with water or milk. It was some years after, in the Highlands, that they learned to carry the flask as part of an angler's equipment. Amongst the pleasures of their stay were the visits paid to the Shepherd at Mount Benger, when much talk took place of poetry, and tradition, and fairy lore, and angling. Hogg was a keen fisher and a subtle observer, and knew the resources of Yarrow and the Lochs, the whims of their fish and all the favourite lures, and he posted his young admirers up in all his local lore. This visit initiated a lifelong association with St. Mary's; and the magnetic recall of the place took effect on my father already that same year, for in September he was back again for a fortnight, fishing for pike in the Loch of the Lowes, where the pike were reckoned finer in quality than elsewhere, and as dainty eating as turbot.

It was not till the next year, 1829, that Professor Wilson made his first appearance at St. Mary's Cottage, with which he was greatly taken, and Tibbie and he struck up a friendship on the spot. Many a convivial gathering followed his advent—the Shepherd an indispensable member of the party. Although whisky was not sold on the premises, it made its appearance there simultaneously with many of the guests, and Tibbie felt free to furnish the hot water, sugar, and spoons. The place was immortalised by providing the scene for one of the "Noctes," and it is also on record that the Professor entertained a number of the county gentlemen at dinner in Tibbie's kitchen, the Shepherd acting as his croupier. Mutton and haggis were the dishes, and the punch-bowl proved enough for dessert, the cooking, dishing, and dining going on simultaneously, while one can fancy what a roar of song, jest, and story made the rafters ring. Alas! the rafters tell nothing, and Willie Richardson "minds it fine, but was just a callant and didna tak' muckle tent."

Christopher North was a prime favourite of Tibbie's, and till the Shepherd's death paid her cottage many a visit. Talking over old days a few years before she died, she said to a lady staying there, "There was mony a ane cam' here, gentle and simple, but I aye likit the Cock o' the North best, that was Professor Wilson, ye ken. I likit him and Mr. Tom Stoddart and Hogg. Eh! but they were the callants for drinkin'! Mony's the time, when they were at it, I've fried a bit ham and took it to them and said, 'Ye'll just tak this bit ham, gentlemen; maybe it'll sober ye;' an' they wad eat it, and just on to the drinkin' again." And then, warming to the old associations, she continued: "Yon Hogg, the Shepherd, ye ken, was an awfu' fine man. He should hae ta'en me, for he cam coortin' for years, but he just gaed away and took anither."

In spite of this little romance of Tibbie's, Hogg was a family man in those days, but was ever the kindliest neighbour to her and all. My father delighted in his companionship, and paid him many a visit both at Mount Benger and Altrive. The vivid imagination of the older poet attracted him strongly, and reacted somewhat on his own; and the "sweet influences" of Nature, to which both were so susceptible, were softening, and to some extent taking the place of, the grim fancies which had preoccupied his boyish thoughts. Yarrow and Yarrow lore had much to do with this development, but Hogg's poetry availed something also. That he was an angler, won my father's ready companionship; that he was a poet, won his devotion. For to the coterie of gifted youths who were his intimates, poets stood on a daïs of more than mortal greatness, and to reach their level was with one and all of them the highest conceivable aim. Their visits to Yarrow in those years meant long days with rod and creel in Hogg's company, and many a homely, hospitable meal at Altrive. In respect of this poet-worship, my father diverged about this time from the canons of criticism laid down by Professor Wilson, and on his own account opened heart and soul to Shelley and Keats, who, coming after Coleridge, were yet to act with him in opening new channels for the imagination and in stimulating poetic impulse for generations to come. It is a proof of the wholesome wilfulness which marked and freshened his nature, that, at a time when men were blind and deaf to their merits, when Wilson called them "poetasters," and the *Quarterly Review* outdid itself in depreciation of their poems, my father read them with delight and felt the full force of their inspiration. That Robert Browning should have been doing the same at this time is natural enough; he was their peer and co-heir of renown; but it seems to me a proof that the lesser poet also had the fine prospective intuition which both heralds and welcomes the coming order.

Some touches of the influence of Keats are

apparent in a long poem in two cantos which belongs to the year 1827, and is called "The Curse of the Dead Sea." Its subject is the grim story of the Cities of the Plain, relieved by the romance of a pair of pastoral lovers called Miriam and Terah. Byron still prevails over Keats, and the nine-lined stanza recalls his favourite form; but the luscious melancholy of the later poet invades the province of sentiment and horror mainly filled by the tale. Two stanzas on solitude in death near the close illustrate this :—

> " Give me a mountain tomb ! a desolate tomb,
>   Where the wild winds shall hush me as they sigh
>   And rustle the dark heaths that o'er me bloom ;
>   Where the young torrent rushes hoarsely by,
>   Watering with spray the rock that lingers nigh,
>   Mossy, and ageless as the stars that shine
>   In the blue oceans of unfathomed sky ;
>   No record chisel and no garland twine,
>   But what in life I loved, in death be ever mine.

> " Give me an ocean tomb ! a foaming shroud,
>   A dark-blue wave to waft me to and fro ;
>   A pebbled shore, a surge that dashes loud,
>   A tide that wanders silently and slow ;

A coral cave that glitters far below
The drifting seaweed and the hollow shell;
Give me the dwelling where the mariners go,
Where wind and wave shall sound my dreary knell,
And the rude rock alone my sepulchre shall tell!"

The verses written during the two next years bear a family likeness to this, and his fancies still wandered in vague wildernesses, and had not found the sure and congenial track in which he achieved his undoubted poetic successes. Ease of rhyme and versification helped a production too prolific to be valuable. The main fact about these years was his delight in poetry and reverence for poets. In the June of 1830 he was again in Yarrow, spending most of his time with Hogg. The Shepherd had contributed a number of articles to *Blackwood's Magazine* called "The Shepherd's Calendar," and these had made the public acquainted with his two wonderful collie-dogs. One day when my father went to Altrive, he found there a clever animal-painter called Howe making a rapid picture in oils of two of their descendants. When the work was done, the

Shepherd asked him to stay to dinner. They dined on Yarrow trout and roast-mutton, and the artist and his host wound up with a brew of whisky-toddy. Hogg addressed his guest from time to time as Mr. Howie, and unfortunately there was another well-known animal-painter of that name. As the toddy mounted into Howe's head, he grew gradually more and more offended at the inadvertence, till, finally exploding with wrath, he started to his feet, clapped his hat on his head, and brandishing his stick at his host, shouted his farewell: " My name, sir, is Howe, not Howie. I am Howe, sir, the animal-painter; the only animal-painter in the world. I don't daub signs, boar's heads and Turks, red lions and green crocodiles, like the miserable pauper you confound me with. Good afternoon, Mr. Hogg; good afternoon, gentlemen. I leave that to correct your ignorance and to teach you that Howe and Howie are very different men." And pointing to his picture of the dogs, he left the house. The picture was excellent, noting every feature of the famous Ettrick collies, and the Shepherd valued it greatly.

Next month my father went with the rest of his family to Kincarrathie House, close to Perth, staying there to the end of September. These summer quarters introduced him to the Tay and its tributaries. In the Tay itself he had little faith as a trouting river, considering its trout both scarce and of poor quality. Its feeders yielded him better sport. He was occupied in autumn and winter with his work at college, and this was taking the definite direction of study for the Bar, his class-tickets for the session of 1830-31 indicating attendance at Professor Cheape's lectures on Civil Law, and Professor Bell's lectures on the Law of Scotland. His holiday hours were devoted as usual to the Muse, and this winter's leisure is responsible for a poem which made some little stir at the time, and which may certainly claim the distinction of being an early product of the Spasmodic School, and one at all events inspired by vivid if somewhat gruesome imagination. With the touch of bizarre originality natural to him, he defied all precedent in its title, and it was published early in 1831 by Henry Constable as "The Deathwake; or, Lunacy: a Necromaunt in three Chimeras."

In "The Deathwake," the poet's imagination, stirred no doubt by Coleridge's "Ancient Mariner," sought the incidents of his story within a range of subjects which excite rather our repulsion than our sympathy. Madness, death's decay, remorse, engross the interest and overwhelm, in the intentional reiteration of their grim and painful details, the tenderer touches which seek to relieve their horrors. Had these conceptions been handled with the power of maturity, "The Deathwake" might have breasted repulsion and gained fame in the vanguard of spasmodic poems; but it cannot be denied that feverishness rather than strength distinguishes the sequence of its incidents, and that extravagance destroys their emphasis. Madness, a passion which demands supreme strength of artistic handling, becomes superb in King

Lear, overwhelmed with emotions which no touch of sensuousness enfeebles; but in the love-sick Julio its wildness and incoherency scarcely impress us even with pity.

The story of "The Deathwake" is that of a monk, who having loved a nun in a neighbouring cloister, finds himself assisting at her funeral. His reason gives way at the shock, and at midnight he exhumes her body, bears it to the shore, and sets sail with it upon the sea. The circumstances of the slow decay of the once-beautiful Agathé are mingled with the details of his strange voyage. At last he reaches an island, on which the nun's father lives as a hermit, in remorseful expiation of the cruelty which forced his unwilling daughter to take the veil. Here, in an interval of sanity, Julio shrinks from the now loathsome corpse and tries to tell the hermit his story. His reason collapses once more in the effort; the hermit flies from his presence, and at night the rising tide sweeps the madman and his ghastly charge from the rock on which he has laid her.

The hermit finds their bodies washed up on the shore, buries them, and picking up a jewelled cross upon the sand, remembers it as a gift to his daughter, realises that he has buried her and her lover, and dies upon their grave in an agony of remorse.

The influences of Coleridge and Shelley are marked, while the passages which treat of the sea at rest or in storm have some suggestion of Byron.

Professor Wilson, writing in *Blackwood's Magazine* four years later, calls "The Deathwake" "an ingeniously absurd poem—with an ingeniously absurd title,—written in strange namby-pamby sort of style, between the weakest of Shelley and the strongest of Barry Cornwall." He goes on to say: "We have good hopes of Mr. Stoddart as a poet,—if he will only be a little more rational, and, after his long and intense study of all the poetasters, will but read one or two of the poets of England."

It is not wonderful that such merits of imagination and poetic expression as may be found in "The Deathwake" escaped recognition from a critic who swept away Keats, Shelley, and Barry Cornwall amongst the "poetasters." As a passage in which these merits are evident, I may quote the opening lines of Chimera II. :—

> "A curse ! a curse ! the beautiful pale wing
> Of a sea-bird was worn with wandering,
> And on a sunny rock beside the shore
> It stood, the golden waters gazing o'er ;
> And they were heaving a brown, amber flow
> Of weeds that glitter'd gloriously below.

> " It was the sunset, and the gorgeous ball
> Of heaven rose up on pillars magical
> Of living silver, shafting the fair sky
> Between dark time and great eternity.
> They rose upon their pedestal of sun,
> A line of snowy columns ! and anon
> Were lost in the rich tracery of cloud
> That hung along magnificently proud,
> Predicting the pure starlight, that beyond
> The east was armouring in diamond
> About the camp of twilight, and was soon
> To marshal under the fair champion moon,
> That call'd her chariot of unearthly mist
> Toward her citadel of amethyst.

"A curse ! a curse ! a lonely man is there
　By the deep waters, with a burden fair
　Clasp'd in his wearied arms.—'Tis he ; 'tis he,
　The brain-struck Julio and Agathé !
　His cowl is back—flung back upon the breeze,
　His lofty brow is haggard with disease,
　As if a wild libation had been pour'd
　Of lightning on those temples, and they shower'd
　A dismal perspiration, like a rain,
　Shook by the thunder and the hurricane !

" He dropt upon a rock, and by him placed,
　Over a bed of sea-pinks growing waste,
　The silent ladye, and he mutter'd wild,
　Strange words about a mother and no child.
　' And I shall wed thee, Agathé ! although
　Ours be no God-blest bridal—even so ! '
　And from the sand he took a silver shell,
　That had been wasted by the fall and swell
　Of many a moon-borne tide into a ring—
　A rude, rude ring : it was a snow-white thing,
　Where a lone hermit limpet slept and died
　In ages far away.　' Thou art a bride,
　Sweet Agathé ! Wake up ; we must not linger ! '
　He press'd the ring upon her chilly finger,
　And to the sea-bird on its sunny stone
　Shouted, ' Pale priest that liest all alone
　Upon thy ocean altar, rise, away
　To our glad bridal ! ' and its wings of grey

> All lazily it spread, and hover'd by
> With a wild shriek—a melancholy cry!
> Then, swooping slowly o'er the heaving breast
> Of the blue ocean, vanished in the west."

Chimera I. has the following passage:—

> "Oh! he was wearied of this passing scene!
> But loved not death: his purpose was between
> Life and the grave; and it would vibrate there,
> Like a wild bird that floated far and fair
> Betwixt the sun and sea!"

The description of Agathé when the young monk first saw her may be quoted as another specimen:—

> "But there came one—and a most lovely one
> As ever to the warm light of the sun
> Threw back her tresses,—a fair sister girl,
> With a brow changing between snow and pearl,
> And the blue eyes of sadness, fill'd with dew
> Of tears,—like heaven's own melancholy blue,—
> So beautiful, so tender; and her form
> Was graceful as a rainbow in a storm,
> Scattering gladness on the face of sorrow.—
> Oh! I had fancied of the hues that borrow
> Their brightness from the sun; but she was bright
> In her own self,—a mystery of light!

With feelings tender as a star's own hue,
Pure as the morning star! as true, as true;
For it will glitter in each early sky,
And her first love be love that lasteth aye!"

Eleven years after its publication, "The Deathwake" was printed in America, appearing in several numbers of *Graham's Magazine*, under the title of "Agatha; a Necromaunt in three Chimeras," and purporting to be by a certain Louis Fitzgerald Tasistro. This piracy did not come to my father's knowledge till 1876, when Dr. Appleton of the *Academy* forwarded to him a letter on the subject from Mr. Ingram of the *Illustrated London News*. He failed to appreciate the compliment which Mr. Tasistro's cool appropriation implied.

No sooner was "The Deathwake" off his mind than he began another poem, with the sounding title of "Ajalon of the Winds." Of this I can find no vestige, except the allusion to it in the following letter from Henry Glassford Bell, which I am tempted to quote in full, belonging as it does to the spring of 1831, and indicating the opinion of the young poet held by a gifted contemporary, who was to prove a lifelong friend.

"YORK HOUSE, HAMPSTEAD, LONDON,
May 30*th*, 1831.

"MY DEAR SIR,—I received, about ten days ago, your letter and poem. I have now read 'Ajalon of the Winds,' and think it on the whole decidedly the best thing you have done, though it is not without the obscurities and exaggerations which distinguished 'The Deathwake.' It is pervaded, however, by a bold dash of original genius, and I think if a respectable London bookseller publishes it, would have a fair chance of attracting some attention. I esteem it so well, that I intend having it conveyed to Lockhart; and if he would take an interest in it and recommend it to Murray, it would appear under the best auspices. Of course I cannot promise that he will do this; and besides, he is at present in Scotland, but is expected back in a week or two. The delay is of little consequence, as nobody is publishing books just now, politics having spread such a panic among the booksellers, that I know of several works lying ready printed in their warehouses, which they are afraid to bring out till the fermentation subsides. Should Lockhart decline recommending your poem, I shall then hand it to some of the publishers myself; but I would certainly recommend that it should be abridged by nearly one fourth, by which means the story would be strengthened and several unnecessary exuberances lopped off.

"I have no doubt your projected treatise on angling will be good. You know the art well; and besides, you will express yourself in an original and striking way regarding it. I never flatter people, as you know very well, but I like your prose style from its straightforward manliness and the healthy interfusion of thought and sentiment. I think you undervalue Hogg's capabilities for writing a book on angling. It would be different from yours, but he would be a dangerous rival to you. We have got some ponds in the neighbourhood of Hampstead, brown and muddy, where people fish for hours together, never moving from the spot, and keeping their eye intently fixed on their motionless float, till at length, toward evening, it dips a little, and they pull out a—tickleback! not quite so large as an ordinary-sized minnow. Nevertheless I like Hampstead much. It is one of the most beautiful villages in the neighbourhood of London, which is only three miles distant, and the walks and country round are enchanting. In the immediate vicinity reside Coleridge, and Joanna Baillie, and Malthus, and Lucy Aiken, and others.

"We contemplate, however, running across in a few weeks to Paris, and will probably visit Edinburgh by September.

"Did you whack any of the *vile pecus* during the late riots? I should have liked to knock in the breadbaskets of the editors of the *Scotsman*, the secretaries of the 'Political Union,' and some other worthy gentlemen. How overwhelmingly appalling was the declaration of some of the constables that they would 'lay down their bâtons' unless Jeffrey were returned for Edinburgh! Only think what would have been the state of Europe if the constables had laid down their bâtons! The threat was enough to annihilate Toryism. A constable laying down his bâton is probably the most awful object in nature.

"Present my best remembrances to your father and mother and Miss Stoddart. Give my best regards also to Professor Wilson and his family when you see them, and believe me yours always very sincerely,

HENRY G. BELL."

In July of this year my father made an extended walking-tour, accompanied during the early part of the month by a friend, but from the 16th to the 28th making his way alone. At first his head-quarters were at Perth, and he fished the feeders of the River Devon, which come from the Ochils. When his friend left, he walked up the Tay to Moulinearn, explored its neighbourhood, fished up the Tummel to Loch Tummel, and stayed all night in the ferryhouse, which was kept by two deaf and dumb brothers. They gave him a Highland supper of oatcake, eggs, trout, and whisky, and a bed of dry heather, and one of them rowed him next morning to the head of the loch. He then walked along the upper river till he reached the head of Loch Rannoch. He slept at the little inn there, and next day fished up the Gawin to Loch Eatach, creeling one hundred small trout on the way. On the following morning early, he started for the Lyon Water across the moor, trackless at that time. Mist settled down with rain and wind, and he lost sight of all the land-marks. He pushed forward bravely, but at the end of ten hours' weary trudge was on the point of yielding to fatigue and of flinging himself down on the drenched heather, when the clouds suddenly parted, the sun outburst as if by miracle, the mist fled in wreaths up the hills, and below him in full flood tore the Lyon Water down a green and sunny valley. Away went fatigue from his limbs like the mist from the hills. In a moment he stood by the river, rod in hand, and late though it was, he did not leave it till he had landed some of its finest prizes. Passing Fortingal and its ancient yew-tree in the evening, he made his way to the inn at Cushieville. Next day he fished the Tay as far as Aberfeldy, and reached the foot of Ben Lawers on the loch, to spend a somewhat dismal Sunday there, his Monday's success on the loch in no way compensating for the halt. Turning off to Killin, he found the Lochy in better humour, and fished it to its junction with the Dochart, from which he made his way by the latter stream to Luib. From Luib he sought the Trossachs, fishing as he went, and then struck up Glen Falloch to Tyndrum, thence making for the Awe up the valley of the Urchay, and came at last to Loch Awe and Dalmally, where his month's wandering ended, and whence he found his way to Inverary, and taking steamer there, went home.

Such wanderings in lingering communion with moor and stream increased his knowledge of the art he followed all the summer months, and taught him many a different secret of the rivers in their valleys, and how and when to woo and win the trout in each. Enthusiastic, dreamy and unworldly, he passed at once into the intimacy of Nature, and found joy there and instruction. He noted and remembered well; and rambles such as the foregoing, solitary and observant, heaped up the knowledge on which he drew afterwards for his practical works on angling, while at the time his enjoyment gave his busy fancy impulse, and one fresh lay followed another; so that before he was twenty-five years old, he had shaped and published in magazine or book nearly all his best angling songs. His Muse cast her tragic weeds when winter was over and carolled gaily in the sunshine by the river. Already, too, he was thinking of a treatise on angling, one which should communicate his acquaintance with the art to those who wished to learn it.

In September and October of the same year he was at the English Lakes. This, except for some visits to London and occasional descents upon Northumbrian streams, seems to have formed his only experience of the English side of the Border; and but for an invitation to stay with the Wilsons at Elleray, he might scarcely have accomplished even this. The district was full of interest for him, and yet he never cared to return to its becks and waters. He has told the chief incidents of his stay in "An Angler's Rambles." John Wilson the younger and he visited every lake and stream on which a fly could play, and the Professor himself made out their chart; but Troutbeck and its "Mortal Man" were the only points on which his memory dwelt in the talk of later years. The famous signboard has long since disappeared from the little hostelry at Troutbeck, although the latter still goes by the name of the "Mortal Man." He met Hartley Coleridge and De Quincey at Elleray, but did not have the good fortune to see Wordsworth. The season was too late for successful fishing, and the Wilsons soon after gave up Elleray; and as his liking for a place depended on his first impressions and his personal associations, the Lakes never tempted him to return.

Towards the end of the year he was admitted as a member of the Speculative Society, to which many of his friends belonged, most of whom were, like himself, studying for the Bar. The young men of his generation who formed the body of the Society and shone in its debates were nearly all destined to distinction in after life. John Hill Burton, William Aytoun, Lord Ardmillan, Professor Blackie were amongst them, as well as many others successful in their day and interesting to each other. The debates were brilliant, and the members were seasoned in giving and taking each other's smart replies. The voices, eloquent and caustic, are hushed now; the one or two which linger have exchanged youth's racy, combative ring for the wise and unregarded monotone of age. My father's intimates at this time shared with him two noticeable characteristics. They were poets and Jacobite Tories. Such late lingering Jacobites were necessarily poets. Only the poetic mind could picture such posthumous politics of romance.

An imaginative allegiance to dead and buried princes, whose fair persons and dramatic fates were their sovereign claim to this æsthetic homage, was only possible for poets. As there was no living claimant for the Jacobite vote, they practically supported what poor Toryism the country could substitute, and were, except for purposes of conversational caprice, very loyal and patriotic subjects of the State.

The winter passed as usual, the law studies making very leisurely progress, while the harvest of summer's busy idleness was threshed and garnered. Angling was making a clean sweep of the fancies and ambitions which had disputed his imagination till now. His "Art of Angling" was begun, and he polished into a finer grace some of the lyrics which had taken shape in

July. At home, his fishing exploits and experiences had willing listeners; his poetry of every kind was scouted. Only his sister Frances cared for it, and, with the vein of satirical wit which distinguished her, her comments were more often critical than otherwise. She delighted in Nature too, and had found expression for her delight with the pencil and the brush, so she gave ear and appreciation to his poems of the rod and river.

There was one ingle-neuk besides the Professor's where he found hearty and sympathising listeners, and was always cheerily hailed as " Poet." This was at Powderhall, a short distance from Bellevue Crescent, where, in those days, Colonel Macdonald, a cousin of my grandfather's, lived and exercised a kindly hospitality. The family group was a large one, including not only the Colonel's wife, but his gifted sister, as well as three sons and several daughters. Young and old were fresh, witty, and unconventional, and welcomed originality in others. The place, too, had its charms—a large, old-fashioned garden, with stone fountain, sun-dial, and fish-pond, with shaded walks and sunny terraces, formed an ideal scene for many a merry gathering of the cousins and their friends. In winter the big fireplaces proved even more attractive, and the circle round them was pretty often sure to include one or other of the Stoddarts. Here my father might rhapsodise as he pleased and read to a chorus of admiration his wildest tales in verse. There was no stint of applause, nor any mortifying doubt of the author's genius. With his fishing poems there was hearty sympathy, for Colonel Macdonald and his sons were accomplished anglers. Here he might be often found taking refuge from disputes at home, for his father and he differed radically on many points. It must be admitted that he spoke his mind too mutinously and gave the Admiral cause for displeasure; but that could scarcely be avoided with natures so unlike. It is on record that one winter evening, after such an altercation, my father flung out of the house with an angry boyish threat that he would drown himself. The threat gave no anxiety at first, but when eleven o'clock struck and there was no sign of his return, my grandfather began to fidget. At midnight his alarm grew uncontrollable, and deciding that the nearest water available for drowning was the pond at Powderhall, he rushed thither, determined to have it dragged on the spot. As he burst into the dining-room, where the habitual late hours were spent, he found the culprit comfortably seated in an arm-chair by the fire, holding forth in rhyme and in radiant possession of the ears of the house. Suicide had faded from his mind at the threshold of Powderhall, and his father may well be excused if his relief took the form of a right royal rage.

The happy days at Powderhall came to an end as "death stepped in and took" one after another of the sons and daughters, and at last only the old people and one daughter survived, never to restore the merriment which once had been part of the very air of the house. Now all are gone, and Powderhall is a restaurant, and its garden a place for public sports.

On the afternoon of the 4th of May 1832, William Aytoun and my father made their appearance at Tibbie's cottage, footsore and weary after a morning at the Tweed and a tramp from Innerleithen. They found the place turned upside down, and the usually hospitable Tibbie by no means glad to see them. "Ye canna bide here," she said, "there's no a room for ye." It turned out that it was her eldest son's wedding-day, and that great preparations were being made for the event, which was to take place in Scotch fashion that evening. The young men flatly refused to be turned off, invited themselves to the wedding, and offered to sleep on tables, chairs, or benches, if they could get no better bed. Tibbie gave way at this, and made them welcome. All afternoon the guests dropped in from Forest farm and hamlet, and when the hour arrived, there came with it not only the minister, but the Shepherd with his maud on his shoulders and a fiddle in its folds. He was master of ceremonies and chief fiddler when the dancing set in, and no better fiddler ever kept a ball going. Supper and whisky were plentiful. Aytoun and my father gave in at midnight, for neither was skilled at reels and country-dances, and they were weary with the morning's walk. They had drunk more healths, too, than their heads were used to, and they crept into bed and fell fast asleep in the very middle of the uproar. Hogg fiddled and the company danced till four in the morning, when a great "skailing" took place in the daylight, and the weary Shepherd rolled into the empty press-bed in the kitchen. But he could not sleep for excitement and thirst, and in the morning his room-fellows were wakened by his shouts for water. He had emptied both jugs in the kitchen, and was bawling, "Tibbie, wuman! watter's terrible scarce wi' ye; can ye no fetch in the loch?"

Aytoun and my father stayed some days at the Cottage, and found St. Mary's Loch in capital trim for fishing. The latter records a take of five dozen excellent trout on the 7th of May. He had been there already in April, but in that month his best take was three dozen and a half.

About the middle of June, John Wilson the younger and he started, with rods and baskets, for a walking-tour which lasted till the 14th of July. It was a zigzag ramble, and had its share of vicissitudes. After visiting the Trossachs, they made their way by Glen Falloch to Dalmally, and thence to Glen Etive, where about nightfall they managed to miss their way, and wandered in rough roads till four in the morning, when they reached King's House. Not a loch nor lochlet, not a stream nor burn, escaped their attention on the way, and my father records with pride the splendid baskets of trout secured by his friend. From King's House they fished the Coe to Ballachulish, and thence made their way to the Lochy, where good sport awaited them. The large trout here made havoc of their fishing-gear, and they had to stop at Fortwilliam and repair their losses. True anglers can easily find supplies, and a few feathers from the innyard, with some threads of green worsted from a ragged carpet-edge, were enough to dress their hooks and furnish them with a new stock of killing flies, which proved their merits with the sea-trout next day. By the Spean they fished their way to Badenoch, halting at Loch Laggan, where the little inn was the scene of an unaccountable drain upon their travelling resources. They went to bed with their purses in a satisfactory state, and in the morning found their contents strangely shrunk, though not entirely abstracted. This brought about a change of plan, and although they hung about Loch Laggan for a day or two, their unwilling faces were peremptorily set homeward.

It was in the autumn of 1832 that Sir Walter Scott died, and his death, associated with the Tweed, which he has made the most beloved river of Scotland, inspired in my father's mind the beautiful lines "To the Tweed," which give early expression and prediction to his own lifelong love for its waters, and enshrine a very exquisite lament for the dead. He never met Sir Walter Scott, although as an Edinburgh boy he knew his figure well going to and from the Parliament House.

Once in the April of 1830, Hogg invited James Ferrier and him to dinner; but such kindly hospitality was so frequent, that they carelessly allowed the morning's fishing to preoccupy them till past the hour, and then gave up all thought of Altrive. Deep was their mortification to learn next day, when they went with their excuses, that Scott and Sir Adam Ferguson had unexpectedly dropped in the day before, had dined with the Shepherd, and had been in most genial mood.

On the 23rd of February 1833, my father was admitted a member of the Faculty of Advocates, but I cannot learn that he ever held a brief. His legal education was of considerable use to him, however, and enabled him to bring both patience and understanding to the study Acts of Parliament affecting rivers and fishing, qualities which Acts of Parliament generally repel. He was busy with the papers on the "Art of Angling," already alluded to, which appeared in 1834 in *Chambers's Journal*, and were afterwards published in book form, running through two editions. It is, perhaps, not too much to claim that this little book was the first practical Scotch manual on angling. Stray papers on the subject had appeared from time to time in Scotch magazines, but a treatise of instruction in the best-known modes of angling in Scotch rivers and lochs was then wanting. The author laid claim "only to scatter his handful of ideas, as he had reaped them from the track of personal experience and investigation." Already he touched on every department of the art, from the angler's equipments to his methods, and the clear and pleasant chapters of information and suggestion were supplemented by breezy angling songs. The little book was heartily welcomed by brothers of the craft, and Professor Wilson gave it a generous meed of appreciation in *Blackwood's Magazine* for July 1835, following it up in the August number by an article on "Anglimania," in which he speaks of "the silent trade, so dear to all thoughtful hearts, from old Izaak to young Tom—in surnames from Walton to Stoddart."

The summer months of 1833 were spent at Crieff, where the family had made their headquarters that season. Two of the four brothers had by this time left the home circle, one to settle for life in Dantzic, the other to follow his father's profession. There seems to have been no prolonged pedestrian tour this year, but many a successful excursion to Lochs Turret, Freuchie, and Earn, and a thorough survey of the angling resources of the neighbourhood of Crieff. In 1834 my father renewed acquaintance with the Tyne in Haddingtonshire, and with the Devon in Clackmannanshire, during a two months' residence at Dollar, thirty of the sixty days being spent at the river-side or at Gartmorn Dam, where he and his youngest brother killed twenty pike apiece in the course of three visits.

September and part of October were spent in Ettrick with his friends the Wilsons. The Professor had rented Thirlestane House and its shootings during Lord Napier's absence. The weeks were winged which were spent in such companionship and such surroundings, and they added to his store a consummate knowledge of the Ettrick in every mood of autumn.

Next year's tour was that which influenced his whole succeeding life. Crieff was once more chosen as summer-quarters by the Admiral and his wife, but its neighbourhood was well known to the now experienced angler; and after paying proper respect to the Earn, he started, rod in hand, for a march through Perthshire to the Spey. He spent some days in Badenoch, pursuing his acquaintance with the country which John Wilson and he had left so summarily three years before; and then, quitting the valley of the Spey, he made for Inverness, and laid its loch and river under contribution. From the Ness he struck northwards to Dingwall, intent upon the Beauley on one hand, and the beautiful chain of lochs which lie to the west of Strathpeffer on the other. Early in July he made his way by the Strath to Contin, where a comfortable-looking farmhouse by the roadside offered rest and accommodation to travellers. Opposite the house, and across the road, was a garden gay with flowers, and beyond the garden stretched a stately pine-wood. He had crossed a bridge over the Rasay, and knew that a mile farther on lay Loch Achilty, with its pine-clad tor, and farther west still Lochs Garve and Luichart, with their feeders and effluents, and the numerous lily-bordered lochlets in their neighbourhood. He knew that the Strath was full of tempting waters, and that Highland proprietors had not yet discovered their value in the Southern market. His rod and he would have kindly access to all, or nearly all; so he made up his mind for a prolonged halt in the cosy farmhouse, which was inn as well. Some girls were playing "bedgels" on the road in front of the house, and as he talked to the handsome old farmer at the door, he turned at the sound of their laughter to watch them for a moment. That moment sealed his fate. They were such a bevy of girls as one seldom sees, tall, straight, and graceful, with faces little short of beautiful; and one of them; "more than common tall," with arched black eyebrows, grey eyes, and a cloud of raven hair, riveted his gaze. The girls had taken no notice of the traveller at first, but finding him rapt in admiration of "Bessadh," they took to their heels like a herd of startled deer and fled round the end of the house. Here was a poet's destiny sprung upon him, as it should be, from an ambush primevally planned. He stayed at Contin about three weeks, making acquaintance, not only with the streams and lochs, but with the family at the farm. It was not very easy to pursue his wooing, because Bessie either took to her heels or relapsed into Gaelic at his slightest advance, and as he was genuinely in love, he had to take the father into his confidence and win his help. Old Mr. Macgregor's help was somewhat misleading at times, as he did not very well understand the young Sassenach wooer himself, and the Gaelic compliments with which he furnished him gave their object a firm impression that her admirer was a lunatic. Time, however, convinced her that he was not madder than reason; and when his stay came to an end, her shyness was so far overcome that her father promised he should marry her after a year, if his parents gave their consent. About thirty years afterwards he commemorated the happy Contin days in a poem called "A Dream of the Past," in which he says :—

> "I dreamt of a circle scattered,
>   Of thy home 'mid the hills of heather—
> Of faces fair that shone out there
>   When we cast our lot together.
> I dreamt of a white-haired patriarch
>   Versed in the Celtic tongue,
> Who took his laugh at the Sassenach
>   That courted his daughter young—

> An ancient 'mong the patriarchs,
>   Who can speak to his hundred years,
> And, though reft of sight, is still in the fight,
>   Still in this valley of tears."

His days at Contin had other incidents than those of love's troubled course. He followed his quest of river and loch with a steadiness which speaks to its power. Perhaps the dreaminess which was always inherent in his disposition led him to carry his romance away from its object to cherish it in solitary musings. At all events, he made good his plan of exploration, and added to his notes a wealth of detail and observation about the rivers of Eastern Ross-shire.

He had ventured one day up the Rasay, with the intention of trying the series of salmon-casts which lie below the beautiful birch-shaded falls of Rogie, when he was stopped from putting up his rod by a tall and pleasant-looking man, who informed him that this reach of the river was preserved by its proprietor. The friendly warning was given in accents which recalled the banks of Tweed and Ettrick, and a little further talk explained that it came from James Laidlaw, the brother of William Laidlaw, Sir Walter Scott's secretary and friend. The meeting on the banks of the Rasay led to an introduction to Mr. William Laidlaw, who was then factor to Mr. Mackenzie of Seaforth and lived at Brahan Castle. Some notes from Mr. Laidlaw show that through his kindly offices my father secured introductions to such local anglers as were versed in the fishing lore of the district. He dined and breakfasted on several occasions at Brahan Castle, and had much interesting talk with Mr. Laidlaw, whom he always remembered with special regard.

It was at this time that he acquired the experience on which was based one of his most popular social accomplishments. On Sundays, when his rod was furled and both leisure and inclination led him to fall in with the custom of the family at Contin, he went with them to the little church where Mr. Downie preached in Gaelic to his parishioners. One Sunday the whole household, father, mother, seven daughters and four sons, along with their guest, drove some miles in a large cart to the scene of an open-air communion service. He was much impressed by the singular solemnity of the occasion, by the pathetic earnestness of the Highland congregation, most of whom had been toiling from daybreak over moor and mountain to reach the place in time, and to whose naturally pensive faces fatigue and tender devoutness lent a wistful solemnity of expression most harmonious with the spirit of the hills around them. The preacher was a man of note in the North, and the tones of his sermon, now gentle and persuasive, now stern and denunciatory, were in such unison with the scene, that, although my father did not understand a word of it, he followed the sounds and varying emotions with rapt attention, and carried away a vivid remembrance of the whole.

He was already a fine reader, and recited poetry with an emphasis and art which were distinctly original; and he practised the sounds which had taken such hold upon him, recalling the preacher's tones and gestures, until he achieved a curiously realistic reproduction of the sermon, not a word of which, except the often-repeated *agus*, was intelligible Gaelic. His ear had caught the burden of Gaelic sound, although his understanding attached no particular meaning to its words; and his quick sympathy had grasped the sense of those varied intonations by which the preacher had wrought upon his hearers, with whose hearts he was in closest touch. The " Gaelic sermon " was his own, and in it he had no imitators. He was chary of the occasions on which he gave it, both because it involved an immense effort, and because he did not look upon it as a comic recitation, and liked to choose his audience. He had a way of fixing his eye sternly on some unsuspecting friend at the table, and bringing his name into a passage, of which all that could be gathered was the fierce wrath that inspired it.

One night, long years after the open-air service of 1835, he was in the *Clansman* steamer, rounding the Mull of Cantyre, with a little knot of friends, of whom I believe the late Dr. Norman M'Leod was one. They were seated at one table in the cabin, while some Mull drovers were loud in friendly altercation at another. My father was induced to give his "Gaelic sermon," and the drovers subsided into silent and devout attention. At the close they expressed themselves delighted. "It wass a goot sermon, ferry goot, and the Gaelic wass peautiful; but it would not be their Gaelic,—the chentleman would be from Ross-shire." Surely their verdict was a testimony to the accurate local character of my father's rendering, as well as to the natural human susceptibility to sound rather than sense.

The "Gaelic sermon" was much appreciated by Christopher North and his friends, and has fleeting mention in one of the "Noctes," where North, on the tide of an invective, confounds all "unknown tongues," and the Shepherd agrees with him, always excepting "sic as Tam Stoddart's."

On the 24th of July, he bade farewell for a

time to Contin and the family which had so suddenly become important to him, and made for the lochs to the west. He has given a detailed account of his adventures by the way in "An Angler's Rambles," and perhaps the only incident which should be dwelt on here is his first attempt at salmon-fishing. Hitherto he had been contented with the pursuit of the "starry-side," and no man in Scotland knew its haunts and habits better; but although he had watched the nobler fish at cruive and fall, and noted its doings whenever he was near a salmon-river, he had not yet dared to arm himself with tackle for its encounter. He carried only a light trouting-rod, a couple of reels with short lengths of line, a store of hooks and floss silks, and, finding feathers as he went, trimmed his flies on days untoward for sport. He had a letter of introduction to Dr. Dickson, whose farm, near Jeantown, lay on the banks of the Carron, and who invited him to stay at the farmhouse. The river flowed past the house, a pool below a cruive-dyke forming its nearest reach, and on the morning after his arrival this pool was astir with salmon and grilses trying to climb the cruive. The chance was too tempting, and, all unfit as was his gear, he tried his luck; hooked three salmon in succession, who severally made off with a hook and some yards of line, and shelved one of his reels. He believed that the shock of surprise at first contact with a salmon made him lose his head and dip the point instead of the butt of his rod, and this seems to happen often with tyros at the sport. He was fortunate enough to catch three grilses during his four days' stay, and had much success with sea-trout. From Loch Carron he crossed over the hills to Loch Alsh, and then by the Glomach and the Shiel finished his eventful tour.

Before him lay the task of announcing his matrimonial intentions to his family, and he seems to have doubted not at all of their glad consent. It was very natural that they should be astounded, for hitherto he had only worn out shoe-leather on the floor of the Parliament House, and the Bar scarcely promised to be fairy godmother to the young couple. Much talk and consultation followed; dissuasion was useless, for whatever may have been the weak points in my father's character, doubt as to his own mind was not one of them. He wished to marry Miss Macgregor, and that as soon as possible. His parents, in spite of some natural irritation, behaved in the end with kindness and consideration. They began to realise that their son's attitude towards life was genuine, however perverse and unpractical they had reason to think it; and they decided that it would be best to allow him a small competency, which would enable him to marry and to settle in some quiet river-haunted country district, where with rod and pen he might make his life after the pattern he preferred. He asked nothing better, and as the conditions of the engagement were fulfilled, old Mr. Macgregor decided to send his daughter for some months to a school at Inverness, that she might get used to the outlandish tongue of her Lowland suitor. She was still there when he returned to Ross-shire, taking up his residence for about three months at the Contin Inn. He arrived early in February 1836, the marriage being fixed for the 26th of April. The Laidlaws and old Mr. Downie, the minister of Contin, helped him through the intervening weeks, and occasionally on a Saturday he was allowed to make a trip to Inverness and to pay a visit to his *fiancée*.

For the rest, he fished over the ground of the year before, and added a full acquaintance with its spring resources to his summer experiences. On the 17th of February he received a memorable gift from William Laidlaw—a hook, some brown hackles, and a length of white horse-tail hair, part of the fishing-tackle for which Sir Walter Scott was looking in the drawer where he found the manuscript of " Waverley," long cast aside. I have tried in vain to trace the history of this tackle, and can only suppose that my father gave it to some importunate collector. I know that he was a frequent victim to the hunters of autographs, who on several occasions " borrowed " from him valuable manuscripts which they never returned.

Mr. Downie married the young couple on April 26th, and they left the Strath for Nairn, intending to make a short stay amongst the rivers of Morayshire. Of these, my father became best acquainted with the Nairn, " the water of alders," but fished the Findhorn several times, as well as the lochs in its neighbourhood. They liked Nairn well enough to prolong their stay for a year, but by that time its attractions had paled, and a great longing for the streams of the South and the neighbourhood of old friends came over him. They lived in lodgings, so there was no hindrance to stay their steps. An invitation came from Edinburgh, and they went thither in May 1837, to spend a fortnight at the home in Bellevue Crescent. It was a trying time for the young wife, but her introduction to her husband's family had the happy result that the Admiral became once for all her staunch friend and admirer, and that from the rest she received then and afterwards unfailing kindness and consideration.

Kelso had for some months been in my father's thoughts, as an ideal stage in the nomadic life of an angler, and he decided to make trial of it at once. It was in June 1837 that he and his wife arrived in Kelso, scarcely forecasting then that their whole after-lives should be lived and ended there. It would be trite to describe this most beautifully placed of Border towns. The Tweed, which grows majestic at its walls, was the magnet which drew my father; and the silvery Teviot with its affluents, the capricious streams of the neighbouring hills, and the lochs that lie in their hollows, helped to weave the meshes which kept him a willing captive all his days. At that time something congenial to the angler's nature breathed in the very air of Kelso. Men and boys, gentle and simple, plied the rod. The river was to those natives of the place as are the mountains to the mountaineer—first in their thoughts in the morning, last at night. In the early hours they hung over the bridge to observe its moods; at midday they returned to gaze and speculate; at evening they went forth rod in hand, or gathered again in contented groups to watch the sunset on its ripples or count the rising trout. This community of anglers boasted its knot of specialists, amongst them Harry Stockwell, Watty Mathieson, John Pyle, Stewart Gray, James Bowhill, and Mr. David Robertson; and my father's name was soon recognised as worthy to be added to this roll.

During his stay in Nairn, he had planned and written a series of sketches in the form of colloquies between the members of an Angling Club. John Wilson and Aytoun had visited him, and made the acquaintance of his wife at Nairn, and I am inclined to believe that the friends distinguished the Sunday spent together by an escapade to a lochlet whose name they never divulged, where they secured such a "take" of trout as anglers say is only possible on Sunday. They had not dared to face public opinion in the Highlands by taking their baskets, so that when it was time to go home, they had to hide the silvery heaps amongst the heather. The tale was never told in all its fulness, although in after-life mysterious hints of some such impious exploit passed between them.

The scheme of the new book was shadowed forth in conclave during this visit. By March my father had carried it out, and was in correspondence with Mr. Pitcairn of the Edinburgh Printing and Publishing Company, to whom he was introduced by a brilliant and valued friend, Mr. W. B. D. D. Turnbull, popularly known as "Alphabet Turnbull."

The little book was published in the spring of 1837, and its illustrations were due to his artist sister. Unfortunately the Publishing Company failed, and a great part of the edition was not even issued. This is a matter of regret, as the sketches, somewhat in Izaak Walton's vein, have a discursive and interesting flow, with just enough of formality in their style to indicate their literary pedigree. The members of the club, who take part in the river-side rambles, frays with poachers and keepers, encounters of wit around the "social jug," songs, monologues, and disputes, are not all recognisable now, but it is easy to discover the author in "Tom Otter," John Wilson in "Jack Leister," and William Aytoun in "Bill Mayfly," while "Wandle-weir" was probably my father's youngest brother, already an effective angler. The book is very scarce, as the first edition was fragmentary, and no second was issued. It is mentioned in the following letter from William Aytoun :—

"EDINBURGH, 21 ABERCROMBY PLACE,
September 30, 1837.

"MY DEAR STODDART,—I regretted very much not seeing you on your emigration from the breechless regions of the North to the more civilised district of Kelso, but I presume you had so much to do during your short stay here, that you were not easily visible to the eyes of the public. You and I are quite becoming strangers, a thing which should not be, and, by our Lady, shall not be; and I pray you to accept this epistle as proof of my determination to the contrary.

Tell me, my beloved Poet, what do you in the South? what new 'Ajalons' do you meditate, or what more of piscatory adventure and song? I read your last book with great interest, which was considerably excited before by the specimens you showed us at Nairn, and as a proof of it, I send you a number of the *Sporting Magazine* containing my chronicled opinion, and wish it every success. I saw John Wilson last night; he tells me that he is a near neighbour of yours, and sees you frequently. I hope he is happy in his new employment, which astonished me much when first announced. I should have as soon thought of John's becoming an astrologer as a farmer, of his driving Charles's wain as standing between the stilts of a terrestrial plough. But who shall control destiny? . . .

"Are there any hopes of seeing you in town this winter? Kelso is surely not at such an unaccomplishable distance from Edinburgh that you could not contrive to pop upon us like a meteor some fine snowy afternoon, and have a cup for auld lang syne. I have now but a dim and shadowy remembrance of your appearance. I can hardly recall the tones of your voice, and have entirely forgotten the idioms of the unknown tongue. Shall these never be refreshed? Will you present my kind regards and remembrances to Mrs. Stoddart, who I hope continues well?—Yours ever faithfully,

"WILLIAM EDMONSTOUNE AYTOUN."

John Wilson had decided on the life of a gentleman-farmer; and as farming in Roxburghshire then, as now, was high, he had come to Harrietfield, near Kelso, tenanted by Mr. Ogden, to study its art. The friends were therefore within easy reach of each other for a few years, a circumstance which added strength to the hold Kelso was beginning to take on my father's affections. That he was at first uncertain of the future, and anxious to supplement his limited income by some appointment whose duties would be light enough to leave him large leisure for the rod and the pen, is evident from the following letter, written to him shortly after his arrival in Kelso. The touches of pathos and friendly warmth which make this letter interesting were characteristic of his correspondent, a man whose devout catholicism exposed him at the time to gross misunderstanding and injustice. His friendship, as well as that of Alexander Wood, afterwards Sheriff-Substitute of Berwickshire, were the result of old family acquaintance, cemented by daily meetings at Parliament House.

     "EDINBURGH, 67 GREAT KING STREET,
       December 20, 1837.

"MY DEAR STODDART,—I feel almost ashamed to write to you and confess myself wholly inadequate to the ceremony of inspecting the date of your last epistle; but I do most sincerely assure you that the reason for my silence consists neither in indifference to your welfare, nor unwillingness to prove by *deeds* that friendship towards you which I feel cannot be suitably expressed by *words*. The main cause of my backsliding towards you and others in this respect is,— my own communing with my own thoughts,—imagining existence and conversation with the few whom I love and regard,—and that atmosphere of feeling (encircling and enveloping both) which makes one dissatisfied with common-world bustle, and yearn towards a place of rest whither I have no pinions to bear me. All this I know to be a grievous error and sin, and I abhor myself for it; but I pray you to accept my confession, and certify my forgiveness by writing to me at all times when either humour or business impels you, and by employing me in everything wherein my small capabilities can serve you. On business I *can* always and *will* always write; wherefore forget me as an intellectual, and use me as a mechanical beast.

"Confound your ideas of road-surveying! Bethink

you of a better office. Why not seek a sergeantry-at-arms, or some such £100-a-year-bringing berth in the Royal Household? Your father's friends are in power at present, and ours I hope will be so soon. 'Think of this, Master Brook.' These offices require only the labour of drawing the salary.

"Poor John Miller is *dead*—Outram *married*. In one year I have lost them as well as Macdougal. The Bar has almost lost its attractions for me; familiar faces have fled; we are 'beggars all.' Commend me to your rib. Very faithfully yours,

"W. B. D. D. TURNBULL."

Sinecures were more plentiful in those days than now; but my father failed to secure one, and I cannot gather that he ever made very strenuous attempts to do so. From one point of view this was regrettable; but his unique local rank as the poet-angler of Teviotdale would have been forfeited had any such office called him away from Kelso. As the months and years passed, he reconciled himself to a life of narrow means, never grudging lost opportunities so long as the Teviot was free to him, the Tweed accessible from time to time, and his home brightened, not only by the presence of her he loved tenderly from first to last, but by the frequent visits of friends whose comradeship was based on mutual interests, which the absence of luxuries could not affect.

For some years his home-life in Kelso was disturbed by frequent change of lodgings or cottage, but after nine restless years he took Bellevue Cottage, in Bowmont Street, as a tenant, and stayed there for the rest of his life. During the years between his arrival in Kelso and his final settlement in Bellevue Cottage, the events of chief interest to him were the birth of a son in 1838, of a daughter in 1840, and of a second son in 1842.

In 1839 he collected the Angling Songs from the "Art of Angling," the "Reminiscences," and the journals in which some had appeared, and adding to their number, published them in a volume, which also included some patriotic, imaginative, and emotional poems. The publishers were Messrs. Blackwood & Sons, and it adds to the literary interest of the book that it was issued from the same printing-press as the first edition of the Waverley Novels. It was dedicated to Alexander Wood. This volume contains nearly all that is best and freshest of his verse, and he made very few additions in after-life to the poems on angling which form its most important and characteristic section. By them, indeed, he stands or falls as a poet; for, while on other fields he has little claim to the bays won and worn by many, here his rivals are few, and their songs hardly awaken such a memory of whirring reel and rushing river for refrain and accompaniment as do his.

Christopher North, so severe on " The Deathwake," spoke in hearty praise of the "Angling Songs." He called " A birr, a whirr, the salmon's out!" and "Bring the rod, the line, the reel!" "among the best angling songs ever written;" and half a century of anglers have not attained to displace them or depreciate his verdict.

The poem " To the Tweed," with which is inwoven an elegy on Sir Walter Scott, he admitted to be "full of feeling and breathed from the heart, though the style of some of the stanzas be rather too Tom Stoddartish." It was somewhat modern for the Professor, and is perhaps somewhat old-fashioned for the reader of to-day; but to Border ears its lilt has still music and tenderness "breathed from the heart."

In this year my father was living in a little cottage which formed part of the buildings attached to the old Grammar School of Kelso, under the shadow of the ruin which represents what must have been the stateliest of all the Border abbeys. The little town had accepted him very hospitably, and as his reputation grew, proved itself capable of granting him a kindly distinction. He was soon a member of its social circle, of its whist-club and fishing-clubs, and he laid the bases of many a friendship and of many a keen rivalry as stimulating as friendship, which, indeed, was only 'war to the hook' on the river and genial fellowship by the hearth.

Mr. David Robertson, whose skill was no whit inferior to my father's, figured chiefly in the latter relation. An old Tweedside angler, he was put on his mettle by this interloper, and I doubt if he ever succumbed so long as he was able to wield a rod. It must have galled him to find his supremacy threatened by a new-comer, who, one afternoon in the year of his arrival, took eleven dozen fine trout out of Teviot in five hours. He straightened his back for battle accordingly, so that their spring and autumn campaigns were part of the chronicles of Kelso. In spring, either angler would rise at a very early hour to get ahead of his rival; but the day was rare and marked with a red letter on which my father left "Davy" behind to mutter wrathfully over a well-whipped water. Mr. Robertson lived in Waverley Cottage, which had been the home of Sir Walter Scott when he was a boy at school in Kelso. A bust of Scott occupied a niche on its outside wall, and is still there, though the cottage itself is enlarged out of knowledge. In those days it was a low, white house, covered with roses and pyrus japonica, having one gable-end turned to the Knowes, at the other side of which my father lived for a couple of years. The rivals were therefore at close quarters during that time, and one watched for the other's going forth; but it is due to both to say, that however keen the contest, even though it sometimes broke out in racy personal invective, it interfered very little with the regard they had for each other. Sometimes, when argument excited the Homeric strain in either, they would have flown to combat worthy of tradition; but friends making truce between them, the anger fell as suddenly as it rose. Once Davy, returning from fishing, found his rival digging for worms, and ready jeers were interchanged. My father could contrive the keener taunt, and Davy, exasperated, seized him by the throat, and went nigh to strangling him. Straight went my father to the Fiscal to prefer a charge of assault against his foe; but in the very act better counsels prevailed, and he went home soothed and unresentful. Often for days they would hold aloof loftily, stung by some such boast or taunt—for there is a childish element of free-spokenness in nearly every angler; but the frost did not last long, and used to thaw in a hearty laugh at themselves and each other.

A number of the letters received by my father at this time were from editors of now forgotten publications, asking for contributions in verse and prose. Others were from men interested either in fishing or the natural history of fish, and seeking from his experience data to confirm their own opinions. All such letters indicate his position as a recognised authority and observer. Amongst them letters inviting him to join the different angling-clubs in the neighbourhood point to his local fame.

He kept up a steady correspondence with his father and sisters, and in 1838 the Admiral paid him a visit at Kelso, when his first child was christened.

Those early years at Kelso were uneventful,

but were rich in the quiet gain which pleased him best. Their records are all of fishing,—pike in the Teviot, trout in the Kale, salmon in the Tweed, perch in Yetholm Loch. John Wilson and he caught thirty-six dozen trout between them in the Kale on a single day; while he fished for pike in Teviot at least once a week during their season, and claimed one hundred and fifty as his spoil in eight years.

Gradually he gathered his perfect knowledge of the neighbourhood—a knowledge carried into minutest particulars, which embraced every field and tree, every fern and flower, every by-path and its features, the very disposition of the stones upon tracks which he frequented. Nor did this knowledge dull his delight in these familiar things; rather they entered into his daily needs and became one with his sense of life. His nature knew neither satiety nor indifference; it had escaped those fatal clauses of the curse on humanity. He paid short summer visits to his parents in their country-quarters during those years,—to Comrie House in August 1842, to Ladhope House in July 1844. His wife and children were with him at Ladhope, and my earliest recollections are of this visit—of the tall, stern grandfather; of the invalid grand-aunt, who ruled the household with a rod of iron from the recesses of an imposing four-poster, from which a fiat went forth for our first whipping; of the artist-aunt who had a studio, and whose tubes of oil-paint fascinated us into the mischief for which the whipping was given.

From Ladhope my father and mother went to the Highlands, taking me with them; and my memory still retains some shadowy scenes of our stay with the grandparents there. The Macgregors had left Contin, and were settled in a small farmhouse on the banks of Loch Garve. I can remember my grandfather's hearty laugh, the "goodies" he used to give me every day, which "grew on the heather" he said, and a visit to the hills on the back of one of his men, to make sure that they did. The visit is noted in

"An Angler's Rambles," where I find that my father got permission to fish the salmon-casts below the Falls of Rogie from Sir George Mackenzie, and to try other parts of the Rasay from Mr. Horatio Ross, and that he made experiments proving the disinclination of salmon to take the fly after surmounting a waterfall both at Rogie and at a small waterfall occurring in Strath Garve.

In 1845 he spent the month of August at Eyemouth, on the coast of Berwickshire, his wife and children with him; and I can distinctly remember many of the incidents of this seaside sojourn, and specially the stranding of an immense shoal of herring-fry, driven to the shore by a pursuing body of lythe and saithe, to which he alludes on page 323 of "An Angler's Rambles." During this visit, his evenings and many of his nights were occupied with sea-fishing, which, however, never rivalled fresh-water fishing in his esteem.

During the winters of these years he was occupied in carefully expanding the notes which he had gathered in the ten years since his "Art of Angling" was first printed. Not only had he gained in these years further knowledge of both Highland and Lowland rivers, but he had extended his experience in the art, and was now acquainted with salmon-fishing, and a successful follower of this noblest branch of the "gentle craft."

Every detail concerning the salmon and its capture was of first importance to him, and the daily opportunities for observation which his neighbourhood to the Tweed allowed matured his knowledge and made him an authority on many moot-points of its history and vicissitudes. His authority was not, however, admitted in those early days, although he lived to see point after point on which he had long vainly insisted accepted in the end, seldom with recognition of his influence in bringing about their acceptance. Those interested in theories regarding salmon acknowledged his power of accurate observation, complimented him by asking his opinion, which he was always ready to state fully and clearly, and relapsed to their own more nebulous views, to forget, when the truth dawned on them at last, that he had been one of the first to observe and record it.

But his skill as a salmon-fisher was apparent enough, and I have heard one of the best anglers of the last generation say that to watch my father play and capture a salmon was to receive a perfect lesson in the art. He had much delicacy of wrist, which gave a certain artistic finish to his handling of the rod and reel when his blood was up in a worthy encounter with a vigorous fish. The same delicacy served him in fly-making, with which he wiled away the hours of unpropitious weather, and in which his skill was sufficiently known to tempt vendors of fishing-tackle to put his name to lures of their own contriving. He was once pressed in an Edinburgh shop to buy an assortment of flies at which no sensible salmon would have looked, on the ground that they were made after patterns by Mr. Stoddart of Kelso.

The work of arranging his notes and putting

them into literary form was to result in "The Angler's Companion," published by Messrs. Blackwood & Sons in 1847; but he relieved his mind from the positive and realistic character of this work by touching up and completing a romance, which, as I gather from an allusion in a letter, he had already begun in Nairn. This was "Abel Massinger, or the Aëronaut;"—a second title which exercised the critical faculty of an old friend much given to malaprops, who exclaimed, when first she heard it, "The Airy Nowt! what for couldna Tom Stoddart hae called it the Mad Bull at aince?"

"Abel Massinger" was published by Mr. J. Menzies of Edinburgh, but printed in Kelso at the office of the *Kelso Mail*. It appeared in 1846, but had little or no success. My father admitted later that "in point of plot the production was a faulty one and crowded with extravagances." The story deals with the misadventures of a young Englishman, who gets into the power of a villainous brigand-chief, whose fortress near Cosenza defied the Neapolitan Government, and formed a rendezvous for all the robbers of South-Western Italy. This man, Schiavone by name, had conceived a relentless hatred to Mr. Massinger's father, whose person he had secured, and whom he kept a mutilated prisoner in one of the dungeons underneath his castle; and this hatred he extended to every member of the family, succeeding by a series of extraordinary wiles in getting hold of one son, the hero of the romance, and in holding him captive in a dismal cell. His first encounter with Schiavone, his escape from the brigand's clutches with the heroine—another victim—the appearance in London of his foe disguised as an aëronaut, his fateful voyage in the balloon, the startling coincidences which brought the brigand on the scene at every descent of the balloon, his final capture by Schiavone close to the crater of Mount Etna, his captivity and his release, form the groundwork of a multitude of incidents as startling as any conceived by the most modern romancers, and chiefly disqualified to take rank with these by their pretension to greater verisimilitude. Most of the tale is told by the hero himself, who occupies the lonely hours of his captivity in writing an account of his adventures, which, through the friendly offices of a priest, eventually reaches the hands of his brother, and leads to an extraordinary and successful attack on the brigand's stronghold. Again, as in "The Deathwake," the author's imagination defies the shackles of even such qualified reasonableness as is expected from romancers, and dealing solely with the natural—for his hint at Schiavone's compact with the devil is evidently an after-thought—he abuses its scope for coincidences, every one of which startles the reader by its uncanny suddenness, and too much suggests the intervention of the supernatural. The wealth of imagination shown is undeniable, but the lack of sober handling depreciates its value in the book.

"Abel Massinger" was my father's first and last attempt at a prose romance. He learned from its failure that the field in which his power told and was respected lay within the limits of his own experience and observation; and although in later life he gave rhymed form to the vague dreams and vagrant fancies which haunted his musings, it was more as pastime for himself than from any faith in their worthiness to please a wider public than the circle of his own friends.

In 1847 he finished his new work on fishing, which was published that year by Messrs. Blackwood & Sons, under the title of "The Angler's Companion to the Rivers and Lakes of Scotland." This book contained all that was most serviceable in the "Art of Angling," of course entirely recast in form and with fuller practical details, while it added to the older stock a large amount of new information, of which perhaps the part of most enduring value was that relating to Highland lochs and rivers. To this day the work is an angling classic in Scotland, and was without worthy rival till 1857, when Mr. Stewart published his "Practical Angler." The latter work, an important guide to those to whom effective and rapid slaying is the chief aim in fishing, does not pretend to take note of those circumstances of scenery and natural details so suggestive to the angler who is pensive as well as practical, and can therefore hardly hold literary rank with the former work. Its advocacy of newer and deadlier methods and lures gave it precedence with the younger generation of anglers, but it can never be esteemed as more than an excellent guide-book, and deserves no place amongst books akin both in kind and degree to the "Compleat Art of Angling." To these the "Angler's Companion" belongs. A follower of Izaak Walton, my father was his heir in exclusive devotion to the sovereign art, to which he paid tribute of all gifts he owned, of time and talents and enthusiasm, pressing into its service, like his master, such powers as have availed to crown it with a literary distinction no other sport has gained. Hunting-songs there are, lays of the forest and the field, gathered one by one from many a source; but what Nimrod of the chase has woven a whole chaplet of songs, into which have passed the fire and dew of inspiration, to honour the sport he follows? Mr. Lang, in his "Letters to Dead Authors," has noticed this kinship to Father Izaak, and has deemed the two worthy to be peers in an angler's heaven.

"The companion we want," said his veteran critic in *Blackwood's Magazine*, "is the 'Angler's Companion.' As a teacher of practical angling in Scotland, we look on Mr. Stoddart to be without rival or equal. What does the book lack? Anything? No, not even '*a simple recipe for cooking a whitling or good trout by the river-side.*' What a smack there is here of inimitable and beloved Izaak!"

In 1842 John Wilson had become tenant of the farm of Billholm near Langholm, where he stayed during the rest of his life.

The duties and interests of farming led him frequently to Hawick, sufficiently on the way to Kelso to tempt him thither when business was ended, so that his visits to my father were coincident with spring or autumn sales at Hawick. It was generally in August that the return visit was paid, and for the next twenty years no summer passed without this interchange. Such a friendship was of great value to both, but especially to my father, as it kept up in memory and association the brilliant companionship of his youth. Through John Wilson he knew the doings and sayings of his whilom comrades, and so kept alive something of their stimulating influence. Lack of means stood in the way of frequent intercourse with them at this time, and intensified the importance to him of these meetings with his friend, as well as of the correspondence between them.

John Wilson married Miss Graham Bell in the summer of 1848, and his first invitation on his return to Billholm as a Benedict was to his old friend. They had not seen each other for a longer time than usual, and the new interest attaching to the meeting, as well as the arrears of fishing adventure which each felt bound to record to the other, gave the talk considerable liveliness.

Mrs. Wilson's presence restrained their mutual frankness for a time, but when she left them, she heard from her room above the voices in the dining-room wax louder and louder, some difference of opinion waging fiercely between the two. She quaked in momentary expectation of a fight, and was on the point of stealing down-stairs to guard her husband from attack, when the door opened, the angry voices suddenly softened into jest and laughter, and the two were soon exchanging repeated and affectionate "good nights" on the stairs. It was their way—a Homeric way—but ending ever harmlessly. Such passing breezes freshened a friendship which there was no vanity in either nature to blight.

Mrs. Wilson soon shared her husband's affection for my father, and his visits to Billholm were all the happier for her advent there. The letters from Billholm between 1848 and 1853 are full of pleasant allusions to old friends. Here are extracts from two which belong to this period, and dealing, as all the letters do, with the "ruling passion," are also of special interest as giving us a glimpse of the veteran Professor, an "anglimaniac" to the end.

"On the 31st of May I left this and joined the following party at Glasgow,—Professor Wilson and Mrs. Gordon, Professor Ferrier and Mrs. Ferrier, Mr. James Wilson and Miss Henrietta Wilson, Sheriff Bell and Miss Bell, and Mr. Blair Wilson. Next morning we proceeded *viâ* Loch Lomond to Luib in Glen Dochart, where most of the party remained for nearly ten days. During the whole of this time the weather was more like January than June, the hills were covered with snow, and the wind blew a hurricane nearly every day. In spite of all this, Blair and I had very good sport (the rest of the party were scarcely ever over the door), always coming home with our creels pretty heavy. I devoted the last two days to salmon, and killed one each day, and two nobler fish 'never bit the sward.' They were the largest I ever caught, and quite the finest, fresh from the ocean."

As neither letter is dated, I can only guess at

their sequence. We know from Mrs. Gordon's "Life of Christopher North" that he spent his last fishing-seasons at Luib.

"I returned from the Highlands last Wednesday week, after spending a very pleasant fortnight with a pleasant party in the 'land of mountain and of flood.' The weather throughout was most beautiful, but more unpropitious for piscatorial purposes it could not have been, and our sport was accordingly very indifferent on the whole. The first week was passed at Luib. The Dochart was nearly as dry as the turnpike road, so none of its Baunches were to be tempted from their holes. Aytoun and I, however, had tolerable sport in Loch Dochart and two smaller meres among the hills, encreeling about three dozen a-piece *per diem* of small but very fine-eating trout. From Luib we proceeded to Portsonachan on Loch Awe, joined by Henry Glassford Bell. The first day Aytoun and I went in the same boat, the Professor and Bell having each one to themselves. A whole day's incessant flogging produced about three dozen of fine trout as the united effort of the party,—most tiresome work. Next day Aytoun and I again went together, each with a trolling rod and a fly one. From nine in the morning till three in the afternoon, we only got about half-a-dozen trout with the fly of the average Loch Awe size, and were just on the point of giving it up as a bad job, when, strange to say, both our trolling lines ran out at the same instant, and in a few minutes more we each landed a small ferox of about 3½ lbs. Aytoun's line had scarcely been let out when he had him again, and after a nice run a very beautiful fish of 5½ lbs. 'bit the sward.' In less than half an hour my turn came once more, and resulted in the capture of another ferox of about 4 lbs., making four deaths in less than an hour. But this was not all; for no sooner had we got the lines out again, than away they went, a heavy fish evidently attached to each. Being near the shore, we instantly landed; but what was our disappointment when both the monsters turned out to be pike! We, however, had the satisfaction of landing them both, 'goodly fish and thumpers,' somewhere about 7 lbs. a-piece. Another of the same species was soon encreeled, and I have no doubt we should have got several more, and not improbably another ferox, but our bait was exhausted, and we had to return to take our ease in our inn, not at all displeased with the day's sport. The Professor and Bell, who had been fishing with the fly only, returned with very sorry baskets. The day after this the Scottish Cavalier and I again joined our forces, and proceeded to a small loch near Portsonachan, by name Trumlie (so it sounds), taking a boat with us, as it is quite unfishable from the side. This loch is absolutely swimming with small trouts, about the size of those in Loch Skene, and I am sure on a favourable day one might with ease kill twenty dozen. On this occasion the wind was so strong as to render the boat almost unmanageable, and the fishing very disagreeable from our lines getting constantly fast in the weeds, with which the loch is quite covered. We, however, spite of all these annoyances, killed fourteen dozen between us. This concluded our fishing."

In 1848 Admiral Stoddart died, at the age of eighty years. By his will, and that of Miss Sprot, whose death occurred shortly before, some addition was made to my father's restricted income.

During the year 1849 he was in correspondence with Mr. Andrew Young of Invershin, who took much interest in the natural history of salmon, and studied the question practically by experiments in their breeding and development. This correspondence led to my father's visiting Invershin in August 1850. Having tasted blood in the River Shin, he extended his tour, first to Loch Inver, where he was the guest of Mr. Dunbar, whom he counted the best-informed and most successful angler of Sutherlandshire, and in whose house he met Mr. Fitzgibbon, better known to collectors of angling books as "Ephemera." Unfortunately, 1850 and the two years following had the reputation of being the worst years of the century for fishing purposes, and the month of August was exceptionally rainy, the only fine days being hot, glaring, and unpropitious. In spite of the weather, the month's stay in Sutherlandshire proved a valuable one, as his acquaintance with the best fishers of the North, and the permissions he received through the Duke of Sutherland's factors, Mr. M'Ivor and Mr. Horsburgh, introduced him to the innumerable lochs and streams of a country which, but for the drawback of uncertain weather, is surely an angler's paradise. He threw a line over every water his zigzag route encountered, tested its denizens, made notes of its features, gathered information from his hosts, guides, and boatmen (which, as much as he could, he confirmed and qualified by practical experience), and so added a definite if summary gain to his already large knowledge of the waters of Scotland.

Here are a few sentences from a letter to his wife, dated August 10, 1850:—

"The Shin is in miserable order,—lower than it has ever been known to be,—and the lower rod-fishings, those on the best part of the river, have recently been let to a shooting-party, so that I had to operate upon the upper streams alone, on a hot day and under the attacks of myriads of midges. I can assure you the veil was well thought of, and is no useless defence; but it is impossible to fish well with it on, as it makes the face so suffocatingly hot. I was out with one of Mr. Young's men, Donald Ross, and in a short time captured three fish, all grilses, a thing to be proud of considering the low state of the river, but more especially as it had been well thrashed before by the great 'Ephemera,' who in three successive days caught nothing, and has taken to his heels. I expect to meet with him on Monday at Loch Inver. Yesterday I got rowed up Loch Shin; owing to the strength of the wind it required two men to manage the boat. I killed a lake-trout of about 5 lbs., and you can tell Mr. David Robertson I used his line for the purpose."

His visit to Sutherlandshire remained one of his pleasantest recollections, and holds the first place in "An Angler's Rambles." It came to an end on the last day of August, when legal rod-fishing expired for the season, and was well employed up to the dusk of that day, when he caught a fine newly-run grilse in the River Shin. The acquaintances inaugurated at this time lasted for many years, and a close correspondence followed with Mr. Young and Mr. Dunbar on the subject of salmon culture and fishing, supplemented by long and valuable letters from Mr. Horsburgh and Mr. M'Ivor. These kept up the record of Sutherlandshire fishing to the year 1853, when a new edition of the "Angler's Companion" was published, an edition enriched by the knowledge of Sutherlandshire lochs and streams gained from the visit of 1850 and from the letters of his friends in that county. This edition, however, moved off with less rapidity than the first, and the book has not again been issued, and is now scarce.

My father's feats as a fisher on the home streams had by this time secured for him the foremost place in the angling fraternity of Tweedside. Some of these feats are mentioned in the "Angler's Companion," but I cannot do better than give an account of two of them which has been kindly forwarded to me by Mr. Michie, a skilful brother of the rod, who was eye-witness on both occasions. The first incident belongs to 1844, the second to some year prior to the Tweed Acts of 1857, which I cannot exactly fix. Mr Michie says :—

"I for one can testify to some of Mr. Stoddart's angling feats which came under my observation, one of which was his taking at least three or four stone weight of trout from the Teviot, with salmon-roe, then a legal lure, and very much used. Maxwellheugh Mill Anna, on the south side of the river, was his swim. I was on the north side, and almost opposite. The trout were taking well that day, and I had caught between six and seven dozen of them, fair-sized, perhaps not in good season. However, that went for nothing with me at that time. I could notice that Mr. Stoddart was taking at least two for my one. It was getting well on in the afternoon when, all at once, he laid down his fishing-rod and seemed to have given up the sport. I had also made up my mind to leave and wound up ; and, being curious to see his take, I came over the bridge down to the Anna, and got over by the mill-lead sluice to where Mr. Stoddart still was. I could hardly believe what I there saw. His basket (a very large salmon one) was filled, aye, *crammed* with trout. The weight could not be less than a quarter of a hundredweight, and nearly as many were lying on the bank, which he had begun to strap up on a strong cord. Of course I expressed surprise as well as admiration at the great catch, when he quietly said, 'Man, if I had not been out of bait, I could have killed as many more ; and to show you something perhaps you never saw before, look here!' He sat down by the river-side, and commenced washing his hands, and I could see the trout actually *nibbling* at his finger-ends—a fact which had to be seen to be believed. He told me many instances of the like, and other strange experiences and feats of fishing which seemed almost incredible.

"Another day, when angling on the same river between the Old Castle cast and Heiton Mill, another favourite cast, I met Mr. Stoddart coming down. He was literally *clad* with salmon and sea-trout; his large hamper was full, and five or six strapped on his rod hanging across his shoulder and down his back, the perspiration streaming down his face and dripping off his beard and hair. I cried, 'Hallo! Mr. Stoddart, what's up the day? You're killing yourself.' He gave a quiet laugh and said, 'I'm doing this to let the beggars see that all fishers are not liars; for the other day, when I had killed eleven fish (more than the half of which I had left with the boatman and other people at Roxburgh), they threw that in my teeth; so of course this will open their eyes to see that what I have done to-day I might have done yesterday.' I think he enjoyed the discomfiture of the unbelieving 'beggars.'"

The meeting with "Ephemera" at Loch Inver, a very pleasant one at the time, led to a correspondence between the two well-known anglers. It was mainly occupied with the history of the salmon, its much-disputed stages of development and their dangers, and the various attempts at artificial breeding which at that time were attracting the attention of experts. My father's interest in these led him to pay the more important nurseries a visit, and his observations at Stormontfield, near Perth, brought him into contact with Mr. Robert Buist, the superintendent of the experiments there. A close correspondence ensued, which added to his knowledge of the attempt, and enabled him to profit by Mr. Buist's experience. He embodied his views on the subject of the "Artificial Breeding of Salmon" in a pamphlet issued in 1854, which excited considerable interest at the time. "Ephemera," amongst others, entirely agreed with the opinions expressed in it, and asked him to contribute a series of articles to *Bell's Life* on the history of the salmon and the necessity for its protection. The latter subject was now occupying the attention of all worthy anglers on Tweedside, and a determined effort was being made to secure the help of the law for the river. My father's knowledge of the subject, and frequent protests against the abuses to which the Tweed was subjected, made his evidence regarding them of value, and I find indications that it was first formally given before a Commission at Berwick in 1852.

The wholesale destruction of smolts and kelts was the subject of his evidence before the Commission and of his articles in *Bell's Life*. Every child who could secure a few yards of line and a hook filled his pockets with parr, a little fish which is much more fearless than the wary trout; while in the autumn season it was a common thing for men to capture and retain from six to fifteen kelts in a day's fishing. The injury of such license to the stock of both Tweed and Teviot was evident, and called for redress, and the two seasons prior to 1852 and that year itself were signalised by a great scarcity of salmon in these rivers. Other causes besides the wanton destruction of the fish at all stages helped to bring about this scarcity, one of the most important being the exceptional weather during the spring, summer, and autumn of the years in question, long periods of drought alternating with floods of great violence. But to the wholesale and continuous slaughter of smolts much of the evil was attributed, and my father shared the opinion of those who condemned the practice. His interest during these years was indeed concentrated on this subject, and numerous articles in Scotch newspapers, besides his pamphlet and the contributions to *Bell's Life*, prove the warmth with which he espoused the protection of the Tweed. The whole matter was at last matured by the Tweed Commissioners, and in 1857 a Bill "to consolidate and amend the Acts for the more effectual preservation and increase of salmon and the regulation of the fisheries in the River Tweed" was laid before the House of Commons, and eventually made law. In June the Bill was in Committee in the House of Commons, and in August in the House of Lords, and my father with a number of other local witnesses attended in London to give evidence in its favour.

Important in its effects as was this Bill, the subsequent seasons showed that, in respect of the annual and weekly close times, its provisions were not yet sufficiently stringent; and the efforts of the Commissioners secured in 1859 a "Bill to amend the 'Tweed Fisheries Act, 1857,' and to alter the annual and weekly close times in the River Tweed."

It is worth a moment's digression to notice that the agitation for the repeal of these Acts, which is at present growing in the neighbourhood of the Tweed, seeks a pretext for its animus against them in the extraordinary increase of salmon in both Tweed and Teviot since they became law, and tries to establish a connection between that increase and the rapid growth of disease amongst the fish. It is asserted that the number of these is out of all proportion to the bulk of water. "The watter's solid wi' fush," says a local malcontent.

My father always deprecated the clause in the Tweed Acts which forbade the use of salmon-roe as bait, and indeed predicted an enormous increase in bull-trout as a result of its disuse. As bull-trout have increased, and are known to be greedy devourers both of the ova and young fry of the salmon, he would, to the extent of that clause, have sympathised with the agitation. In other respects he believed the Tweed Acts to be useful in their working, but too lenient with regard to the annual close time.

Part of the summer of 1854 was spent at Pitlochry, which gave my father an opportunity of revisiting the Tay and the Tummel. His youngest brother had returned from New Zealand, and was his companion on this occasion, and together they thoroughly searched the district, confirming their opinion of former years, that neither these rivers nor the lochs connected with them can bear comparison from an angler's point of view with the Tweed and Teviot. Their experience excepted Loch Broom from this inferiority. And here my father achieved a success which pleased him greatly at the time, and which he has mentioned in "An Angler's Rambles." He had chosen his flies with an artistic reference to local colouring, a choice much condemned by a native expert, who recommended a trial of his own "fail-me-nevers." These were excellent flies, and favourites also with my father, but, with the wilfulness of intuition, he rejected them, and caught seventeen fine trout, against one caught by his rival, who was accustomed to the loch.

During the winter of this or the next year, he was invited to give a public lecture in Kelso, and chose "Eloquence" as his subject. After drawing a distinction between the inspiration which directs the language of the poet and the acquired and fostered art which directs the language of the orator, he spoke at some length of the three great fields for modern oratory, the political platform, the pulpit, and the bar, and concluded with examples of enthusiasts whose singleness of purpose and unbending will lent to their words so impressive a force that they drew the makers of history into the vortex of their influence, and became mighty factors in the development of human progress. The lecture was no bad illustration of the eloquence which it celebrated; it received a kind of local ovation, and was repeated in some of the neighbouring towns.

Its success led to an early request for a second lecture. In this, to which my father gave the title of "The Union of Love with Truth," he insisted upon a recognition of the sacred character of the whole body of truth, not only religious and moral, but also social and scientific,— an admission of its comprehensive sanctity very rare in those days. With characteristic courage, too, he accused statesmen and clergymen of distorting truth by unduly magnifying the part at the expense of the whole, and indicated the discord and chaos which their limitation had produced. I doubt if his audience appreciated his meaning, and indeed remember that the lecture was counted " havers." Its suggestions would seem mere truisms now in country-towns as well as in capitals. My father did not resent the failure of his second lecture, and indeed could laugh heartily at himself from the provincial point of view, as well as stoutly maintain his footing on the higher and universal ground.

The death of Professor Wilson in 1854 caused the first blank in the circle with which the memories of his youth were most involved, and he felt it deeply. In 1856 his younger son left home to become a sailor, and, except for short holiday intervals, never returned to Kelso. These first losses gave melancholy presage to a nature in which affection played a leading part, and the more because his youth and early manhood had been so little clouded by sorrow that he was unversed in its significance. The ten succeeding years brought that fully home to him; but so far his life was happier than most lives, in that, except by absence, those of his own household, the nearest and dearest, were spared to him throughout.

In June 1857 occurred his visit to London as a witness before the Parliamentary Committee on the Tweed Acts, and in this visit he was accompanied by his wife. Together they enjoyed some of the season's gaieties, receiving many pleasant attentions from old and new acquaintances. These included a box for some Italian Opera, on which occasion my father fell fast asleep. He had just enough appreciation of operatic singing to found upon it one of his most amusing displays, which was a very suggestive reminiscence of the shrill woes and warbled joys of the then fashionable Italian Opera, for which he ingeniously used as sole libretto the word "Abercromby."

It was in this year that Stewart's "Practical Angler" appeared, and, while exciting his admiration as the work of a genuine and skilful fisher, was the means of occasioning him a not unreasonable surprise when he found a certain number of the critics rating it higher than his own works. Humorous allusions to this occur in John Wilson's letters, and the two friends dubbed Stewart the "Pretender."

My father had tried his methods and advocated them long before this, but the mere monotonous slaying of trout scarcely represented to him the sum of gain to be derived from a day's angling. Compliance with the humours of the day, experiments suggested by the scene, methods for every mood, long halts for musing; sometimes a sonnet that must needs be made, sometimes a snatch of sleep on the sunny bank; often a pause for some keen, silent watch, as bird, fish, otter, fox, or weasel enacted its little drama for his delight; a digression to pluck the first primroses or forget-me-nots, which, thrust into his creel amongst the trout, suffered somewhat from their neighbours—these made up the angler's gain, and sent him home smiling and content, whether his basket were empty or full. When it was full, there was indeed a keen enjoyment added; but except in the height of a rivalry, the companionship of Nature requited when the river failed to reward him.

There was, therefore, some room for his surprise at the change in opinion which could exalt rapid and dexterous slaying as the one requisite in angling; and he began to realise that here too the old order was passing, and that the whole-hearted angler of the Arcadia which Izaak Walton had conceived and he had helped to create was giving place to new men,—persons who did other things, who left their banks and offices, and studies and shops, for a day's fishing now and then, and, with good equipments and the "Practical Angler," whipped up some stream and filled their creels, and went home jocund but not a whit more wise.

Some correspondence with Mr. Stewart led to a challenge from the old anglers to the new,

John Wilson and Mr. Russel, the editor of the *Scotsman*, joining the contention, the former on my father's, the latter on Mr. Stewart's side. It was arranged that all four should meet at Tibbie's classic tryst at St. Mary's Loch, which, with the Meggat and Douglas Burn, was to be the scene of the competition. Each pair was to pursue its own methods. Much correspondence passed on the subject, but I cannot discover that the meeting ever took place. If it did, I suspect that the "Practical Angler" won the day.

The Tweed and Teviot fishing-clubs, which had at first enrolled my father's name as member, had by this time requested him to become in one case president, and in the other secretary; and some of his time was willingly spent in attending to the duties of these honorary offices, one of which was to take the chair at the annual dinner of each club, a duty always willingly and genially performed.

Besides these, there was a club of a more private character to which he belonged. This was in existence for twenty-five years, and was known as the Mowhaugh Club. It was instituted by Mr. Elliot of Galalaw in 1845, and only that gentleman's intimate friends had the privilege of membership. He rented a hill-farm amongst the Cheviots, to which he paid frequent visits, which was the scene of the Club meetings. These took place once a year, and were always held on the Queen's birthday. That festival falls at a most favourable time for trout-fishing, and was made the pretext for a delightful day amongst the hills. The morning start was made early, as Mowhaugh lies twelve miles away from Kelso. Once there, the anglers drew lots for the different parts of Bowmont Water, levied sixpence from each to make a sweepstakes for the most successful, and dispersed to fish till dinner-time, while the lay members wandered over the hills and inhaled the fragrant, drowsy air of the Cheviots. As dinner-time neared, all returned to the house, the spoil was weighed and the sweepstakes adjudged, the finest trouts went straight to the frying-pan, and the solemn business of dining began. The long light of early summer soon tempted the diners into the open air, and strange whispers of a pig-chase and other unaccustomed frolics have reached the astonished ears of their fellow-townsmen; and rumours, too, that the pigs were never caught, but taking to the hills, fled into their recesses, and haunt them to this day. Then, over the parting tumbler, songs were sung and stories were told, and my father would give his Gaelic sermon and "Abercromby," and would illustrate the pulpit oratory of his time with the alphabet, or recite his poem "A birr, a whirr!" When the light began to wane and the moon to rise, the members climbed into their gigs and dog-carts, and the procession homewards began, shortened at many a cross-road, as one after another, with friendly shouts and farewells, turned off towards his home. There were thirteen members, and now just three are left, the kindly host and two of his yearly guests.

Nearly all the month of May 1859 was spent

by my father in John Wilson's company. Together they fished the rivers of Dumfriesshire, storing experience and observation. They paid a visit during part of the month to their old friend Sheriff Trotter at Dumfries, and this gave them an opportunity of going to Drumlanrig to see Mr. Shaw, whose experiments on the river Nith had excited my father's interest. Of this day at Drumlanrig he gives a detailed account in "An Angler's Rambles," the ingenious salmon-trap in the Nith, and Mr. Shaw's successful introduction of grayling into that river, being fully described. The Nith seemed to both of the friends of inferior rank as a trouting-stream, and that before the grayling had time to affect the supply of trout, as they are now believed to have done.

Towards the end of the month the friends were the guests of Mr. Macdonald of Rammerscales, with whom they spent a day at Lochmaben netting the Castle Loch, in hopes of securing some specimens of its celebrated little fish, the vendace. They failed in this, although of pike, bream, and eels they caught plenty. Three years later, at a meeting of the Vendace Club, my father succeeded in seeing and tasting this rare and delicate little fish; which, feeding on minute forms of life, can only live where the water abounds in such, and which thus escapes the dangers incurred by fish which take the fly or worm. It runs its own risks, however, for the pike pursues it, and refuses all coarser prey in its neighbourhood. Its delicate form and the transparent heart-shaped patch upon its head, through which its brains may be seen, give it distinction among the different fishes of Lochmaben. Of these fishes, there is a collection, formed by Mr. Archer on the occasion described above, in the Edinburgh Industrial Museum.

Next year brought losses to my father, first in the death of his mother, and then in the departure of his elder son for New Zealand. The latter was his father's true disciple, and took with him to the colony not only much knowledge of the art of angling, but also a deep interest in fish-culture, which has made him a practical and valuable member of its Acclimatisation Society.

The home-circle was greatly narrowed now, but at the same time its resources were considerably enlarged, and for the last twenty years of his life my father lived in easy circumstances. This gave a spur to his natural hospitality, and allowed him also to move about more freely; so that, although the loss of friends, in addition to some of the ills to which the angler is peculiarly exposed, was now reminding him of the passing years, the absence of anxiety and the attainment of many comforts let him down gently, and gave him cause for renewed content. He was still as zealous a fisher as ever, seldom failing to spend four days of every week beside some neighbouring river, and chiefly *in* it; and this in spite of many warnings—severe chills and attacks of rheumatic pain, intensified into lumbago and sciatica.

John Wilson had sent his daughters to a school in Kelso, that they might be near his old friend and convenient for his own frequent visits to Tweedside. They were bright little girls, with their full share of the Wilson beauty and vivacity, and they spent many a holiday afternoon and evening with their "Uncle Tom," taking a quaint and precocious interest in his pursuits. To their presence in Kelso he now owed very frequent visits from their father. Mr. Wilson scarcely bore his middle-age so lightly as his friend. He was of heavier build and stouter, but could still enjoy a day's fishing or otter-hunting, and was the best of companions over the evening tumbler. He was a very handsome man, growing perhaps a shade less energetic, but kindling into delightful talk and racy repartee when the day's exertions were over and supper was on the board; and surely of the simple unswerving constancy of antique times no nature ever showed better example than his.

It must have been during the hunting season of one of those years that a poor hungry fox, which had escaped the hounds the day before, stole into the house early one morning, when both gate and door were open, and took refuge in a corner of the pantry, from which his entrance dislodged a pile of dishes. The clatter summoned the servant, who was much disconcerted by the fierce grin with which the unexpected visitor greeted her. She closed the door and called two workmen who were passing to her assistance; and when my father came downstairs, he entered upon the last tragic scene of the poor "tod's" life. It was a case of justifiable vulpicide, but his friends twitted him with uncousinly conduct. "When a 'tod' comes to visit a Tod, the least he can do is to give him food and shelter," they said. "I will give him both," was the quick reply; "for I have sent him to Brotherston to be stuffed, and after that he will have the shelter of my home."

The incident is trivial enough, but it interested my father greatly at the time; and the "tod," a very large one, had a place of honour in the cottage lobby for the twenty years that followed.

His gift of rapid repartee was well known and

much appreciated by his friends, but a touch of antiquity already separates the instances on record from present sympathy. One impersonal flash may be spared from the past. Some members of the Kelso Reading-Room were discussing a magnificent break of 620 made at billiards by Roberts. "What a time it would take," said one of them, "and how hungry they must have got!" "Perhaps," said my father, "they broke fast."

He took some pleasure in dealing a sly blow at clergymen, who, excepting certain individuals for whom he cherished warm regard, were not highly placed in his favour. Late one evening, at a public dinner, the chairman sent him a note asking him to propose the "Clergy of all denominations." He scrutinised the paper closely, then rising to his feet, said, "Mr. Chairman and gentlemen, I have left my spectacles at home, and may therefore be mistaken as to the wording of the toast which I am called upon to propose; but so far as I can read it, it seems to be 'The clergy, of all abominations!' His *mot* was received with roars of laughter, in which the ministers present could afford to join.

His prejudice against the clerical body included no vestige of hostility to the creed of Christianity. Indeed, his grievance against them was that they displayed a want of reverence for its truths, and an assumption and presumption unbefitting the humility which these enjoin. He objected to have spiritual waters from the Eternal Source dealt out in vessels of such poor size. Their lack of intelligence and sympathy repelled him. For clergymen who held themselves modestly as men and gentlemen, who in their capacity of teachers expounded and explained God's law and love without narrowing and misrepresenting either, he had a deep admiration and regard; and to such he would speak intimately and often of spiritual things—things which occupied a larger share of his thoughts than of his words.

In the summer of 1861 he paid a visit to the Spey, accompanied by his wife and daughter, and took quarters for some weeks at Fochabers. He was much disappointed with the Spey, both as a salmon- and as a trouting-river, and was disposed in after-life to discredit all vaunting on the part of its admirers. He left Fochabers in August, and went to Huntly, where both the Deveron and the Bogie better answered his expectations—at all events, as trouting streams.

No doubt the Tweed had spoilt him for fully appreciating either the Tay or the Spey, and the ease with which it may be fished had by this time disinclined him to struggle with the natural obstacles which are characteristic of the Highland river, and which in his younger years would have added zest to the sport. True, there was no stretch of the Tweed to which he had free access; as to the Teviot, the fishings of the former river belonging to riparian proprietors, by whom they are sometimes farmed at costly rents; but both the owners and the season's tenants kept him in remembrance. Especially to the late Duke of Roxburghe he owed his happiest days on the river. Every spring and autumn the thoughtful invitation came to fish the Tweed at Floors, generally for two succeeding days, often for more; and it is not wonderful that, knowing so well a reach of river unrivalled for beauty and unfailing in its yield, his appreciation of other streams grew dulled.

Nearly every salmon-fisher who came to Kelso sought him out; and his lore was cheerfully at the disposal of these pleasant transient friends, to whom he owed many a day of exciting sport. Amongst them I remember the late Professor Fawcett, who for some years came regularly to Kelso to profit by the Duke of Roxburghe's permission to fish the Tweed, and who during his stay always spent an evening with my father, entering into the subject of angling with enthusiastic interest, and discussing it with the healthy thoroughness of knowledge which distinguished him.

The conversation at Bellevue Cottage did not range over a wide area. There were two absorbing subjects, angling and poetry, and angling took the precedence. For politics my father had little patience. He was contented with being a Tory, and at election times had spasms of fierce Toryism. It is even on record that he boldly tackled Mr. John Bright at a Radical meeting. "Alone he did it;" but he refused to ruffle his mind from day to day with the wearisome pettiness of party contest, and only grew alive to the political situation when it became dramatic, as at election times or under the shadow of war. He did not belong to this age, fevered as it is with humanitarian zeal, over-peopled, emulous, mischievous, exhausting, but to a dream-age of his own, in which rivers filled the meadows with rejoicing and spirits still outnumbered men—and from this he descended to the real world as to Bedlam, to be escaped from at every opportunity.

It was in Teviot that he caught his largest salmon, which turned the scales at thirty-two pounds, and was landed after a vigorous run of half an hour. His biggest prize in Tweed was twenty-eight pounds in weight. On the whole, his captures were not of uncommon size or number. It was more his unquenchable eagerness that distinguished him from other anglers than his success, and it was his gift of finding the most varied expression for his enjoyment which now separates his memory from theirs. Sometimes, on the night before a day on Tweed, he could not sleep for excitement; and an old friend of his reminds me that, one morning in early summer, my father roused him up at three o'clock by tapping on his window—an upper one—with the point of his rod, and hailing him out to fish. There was no help for it, so down he came. "I could not sleep," said his rather early visitor, "for thinking of the Teviot." The two went up the river together. "Yonder!" said my father, pointing into the distance, "come when I will, there's a rascally poacher in front of me." "No, no, man," said his friend, "there's nobody before us to-day." "Do you mean to tell me you can't see his basket?" insisted my father, and then burst into contented laughter when the "basket," proving to be a sheep, rose up and walked away.

My father spent the first fortnight of July 1862 in Galloway, fishing the Dee and the Ken, the Dee impressing him as a river of varied capabilities. The last weeks of July and the first week of August were passed at Eyemouth, the nights being often devoted to sea-fishing. His younger son had returned from his first cruise, and was his companion in these expeditions. They chartered a punt for day-fishing, and made a sufficient number of experiments to warrant the opinion that on our coasts the methods and resources of sea-fishing are very imperfectly understood, and that the whole question presents extensive possibilities. As sea-fishing has not yet received *cachet* as a sport, it lacks the benefit of general interest and of the observation and ingenuity which men of leisure can afford to give. The ordinary fisherman supplies the market, and is indisposed to look further than the great risks which that involves. If his experience includes the glimmering of some new suggestion, he dismisses it as impracticable or hopelessly troublesome. "Donald," said a lady last summer in Skye, "I pay you every week to bring me fish, and what you bring is so coarse I can scarcely eat it. And yet Mr. E. passes the door every day with all kinds of beautiful fish, so I know they are to be got." "Aw, an' I weel believe it," said Donald; "the poor chentleman wull just be making a toil of it."

From Eyemouth my father accompanied his son to London, and spent three weeks with him there; but the visit was devoid of any special interest, and was indeed wholly for his son's sake.

In February of 1863, he brought himself within reach of the law by catching and keeping a grilse which the water-bailiff declared to be foul and unseasonable. Such fish were often taken, and were no doubt often retained, and it was necessary for the water-bailiffs to earn their wages by an undaunted display of determination with the poachers. The presence of this shady fish in my father's creel offered them a brilliant opportunity. The bailiff demanded that it should be flung back into the Tweed. My father said the fish was no fouler than reason, and that he would keep it. The bailiff grew imperious, and my father's blood went up. The fish was not a foul one, he said, but were it black as Tophet, he would keep it. Others came upon the scene and took sides, so that both fish and quarrel remained as dubious as ever. The question went to court on Wednesday, March the 4th, before four Justices of the Peace, and my father got the benefit of the doubt which lingered about the character of the fish. The case made much local stir, as it brought the working of the Tweed Acts into notice and discussion. The trial lasted five hours, and during the whole time the hall was filled by a crowd of eager listeners, who broke into applause when the decision was given in favour of their well-known fellow-townsman.

Evidence on his side was furnished by two of the Kersses, members of the most notable and experienced family of fishermen on the Borders, who could certainly pronounce better than most men at just what fine shade of sombreness the legally clean fish passed into the legally foul.

In 1864, my father was engaged in a lengthy correspondence with his son about the chances of exporting trout and salmon ova from Scotch rivers to the New Zealand streams. Some of his letters were published in the Colonial newspapers; but at that time no steps were taken towards a practical trial, although Colonial agents in London were willing to promote an experimental exportation. Since that time the ova both of salmon, river trout, and Loch Leven trout have been successfully shipped and acclimatised; and the fish-breeding establishment of the New Zealand Acclimatisation Society contains at this time about 700,000 ova of these and other fresh-water fishes, including Rhine salmon in various stages of development.

To this year also belongs a correspondence on a case in which my father took a deep interest. This was the claim made by Mr. Scott of Rodono to a share in the proprietorship of St. Mary's Loch, which had from time immemorial been reckoned as belonging to Lord Napier. My father had fished the two lochs for nearly forty years without once hearing of the rights of Rodono, so that his testimony was considered valuable by Lord Napier and his advisers.

His thoughts had been of late a good deal occupied with these ever well-remembered scenes of his youth. One after another of his comrades there was passing to "where beyond these voices there is peace." James Ferrier, William Aytoun, John Gordon were gone, one quickly following the other; and although he had seen little of them since their ways in life had diverged, as they left the leisure of youth for the pressing forward of manhood, still their figures, unaged and undimmed, peopled his loyal recollections. Now, too, the friend whom he esteemed the best, and who in the rare attribute of constancy, which we expect in God and wonder at in man, was endowed equally with himself, was sinking month by month into the lethargy of an illness from which he was never to recover.

Thinking of them and of past days with them, he was busy putting his memories into shape and writing a series of articles, first for *Bell's Life* and then for *The Field*, in which, while angling formed the main topic, the old friends belonging to every scene, as well as many incidents of their fellowship, found a place.

These were eventually collected and published in 1866 by Messrs. Edmonston & Douglas. The prose sketches were relieved by a selection from his "Angling Songs," as well as by a few new poems, composed for the volume, but scarcely reaching the high-water mark of his earlier tide of minstrelsy. The title of the book was "An Angler's Rambles and Angling Songs." It was favourably reviewed, but did not attain a second issue, and is now scarce.

Some of its chapters are of great interest, particularly those relating to fishing in the neighbourhood of Edinburgh in the early part of this century, and those commemorating his visits to St. Mary's Loch.

Before its last pages left his hands, he had to record a blow from which he never entirely recovered. John Wilson, after two years' gradual decline, died on 27th November 1865. Patient and gentle to the last, in spite of the slow failure first of his bodily powers, and then of the bright wit which made his talk as bracing as sunshine, he left only passionate mourning behind him; and I have no hesitation in saying that his death was the paramount loss of my father's life, and that, although the latter survived his friend for fourteen years, its abiding sense clouded their summers for him, and dulled even the joyous rush of his favourite rivers. From that time his shoulders, rounded now and stooping somewhat from the accustomed weight of the angler's creel, drooped more and more; an unwonted sadness stole into his expression, his step began to lag, his eagerness in fishing to wane, old age to claim him prematurely as his own. Thus he ends the "Angler's Rambles:"—

"But the crowning sorrow was still in reserve. Following hard upon these bitter losses, has been the recent removal, from a home made dear to me as its annual visitor by many a fond association, of the companion in hundreds of rambles over moor and mountain, by the loch and riverside, of a true, generous-souled friend, endowed with qualities of mind far above the common order, possessed of a fine taste in arts and literature, a sportsman whose keenness was of that kind which showed more delight in the success of another than his own; a naturalist trained as such at the foot of Gamaliel, who entered with spirit into the study of zoology, and was well versed in all its branches; one, I shall only add, who, irrespective of any regard entertained for him as the eldest son of Christopher North, was valued, loved, and idolised by all who really knew him; for a more unselfish nature never breathed, and a nobler yet gentler heart never throbbed."

My father and mother spent three weeks of February 1866 in Edinburgh, where they revived some old and made some new acquaintances. Amongst old friends, they met Mr. Glassford Bell, and the renewal of friendly intercourse with him led to a plan for a fishing-tour in Sutherlandshire together in the following August. As a first stage towards its fulfilment, we went in July to Inverness, where my father waited for his friend, and in the meantime made the acquaintance of Dr. Carruthers, at that time the foremost literary man of the Highland capital, and the best fitted to be his companion in either angling or antiquarian expeditions. When the Sheriff arrived, they left for Sutherlandshire, and being favoured with beautiful weather, fully enjoyed the fortnight which they spent there.

I remember that they planned a kind of diary of the tour, which was to be fashioned into a series of short papers, each followed and completed by a sonnet, and that they proposed to call it "The Zigzag Papers," each angler contributing alternately. The plan fell through, however, although it formed the subject of some correspondence afterwards.

It was in this year, too, that Mr. Cholmondeley Pennell, the editor of the *Sporting Gazette*, and an author and sportsman whom my father highly esteemed, began a correspondence with him, which resulted in his writing a series of articles on angling in Scotland for the *Sporting Gazette*. These, as well as similar articles in Kelso newspapers—for one of which, the *Kelso Mail*, he was in the habit of writing an annual review of the Tweed fishing-season—occupied his evening hours, and alternated with numerous poems, no longer fully poetic, in which it was second nature to him to embody his opinions and aspirations.

On days when he did not fish—more frequent now than formerly—he walked, every afternoon in winter, and every evening in summer, up the banks of the River Tweed to where the Teviot joins it, and then past the old mill to Teviot Bridge. His pace was the slowest saunter, and when I was his companion, which was very often, our entertainment was childish enough. He would start a subject and metre, and challenge me to outdo him in lines and rhymes. A foreknowledge of failure did not daunt me, as the contest was exhilarating, and had its gain in our mutual enjoyment. The ease with which he found rhymes was aided by considerable audacity, and led to many grotesque performances. Such improvisations are in their nature fleeting, and although we never wearied of the amusement, we indulged in it without prejudice to our memories. I can only remember one poem which owed more than a fugitive existence to these walks up Teviot. It was at the time when the cattle-plague was much discussed under the name of "rinderpest," and it occurred as a subject for our rhyming duel. But it roused the dormant delight in mysterious horrors which had occupied his early imagination, and his very first line struck too solemn a chord for my more trivial strain.

"Whose herdsman, gaunt and evil-eyed? ..." he began, and I was dumb. He liked the line and held to it, and wrote a weird poem on the rinderpest, which was afterwards included in a collection of his later verse under the title "Death's Herdsman."

In the evening, when supper was over, his desk was put on the table, and for two hours his pen was busy. The habit of seeking daily expression in writing was one acquired in boyhood; and although much of what he wrote was destroyed, and much of his later work was overweighted by cumbrous phrasing, his steady resort to it proved the characteristic, if not very practical, vitality of his mind. He had a native indisposition to prescribed work, but by no means the natural indolence of which he accused himself. Although a great many men would call him an idler, the few men capable of appreciating his powers, and the conditions which alone were favourable to them, would admit that he wasted far less of his time than those who make haste to be rich. The proof was in his unfailing content. "My life," he wrote a few weeks before he died, "has abounded in happy passages. I have been blessed with a joyous and loving wife, attached children, many genial friends, many endearing associations and delights, also a competent income so far as my wants in that direction extend. What more can a man desire?"

The remaining years of his life were to pass tranquilly enough, marred somewhat by failing strength and by increasing ailments of a kind which could be traced in great part to constant wading. He spent a portion of the summer season of 1868 and of the six following years in the West Highlands, making his head-quarters at Oban. His earliest attraction to the West was an invitation from his cousin, Mrs. Cheyne, who was proprietor of that part of the island of Lismore bought after her death by the Duke of Argyll. My father and mother paid her a long visit in the summer of 1868. Lismore serves as the centre of a superb ring of western hills, and the magical effects of summer sunsets and a twilight which scarcely deepens into dark, added to its rich pasture-land and wealth of wild-flowers, make the lonely little island a singularly refreshing summer-haunt. At the foot of the long barrow which forms its backbone lie two lochs, one of which is rich in large red trout, while both of them are eerie even in daylight, and shunned, when the twilight gathers, by the islanders, who mutter strange, half-fledged superstitions about them. My father very soon explored the little territory, fished its lochs, and boated round its coast late into the night, catching lythe and saithe. When he left Lismore, he found himself so enamoured of the West that he took rooms at Oban for the rest of the summer. Here he made an acquaintance which ripened soon into a hearty friendship. It was with Mr. David Hutcheson, then the proprietor of the line of steamers which has opened up the West

Highlands to the world of summer-tourists. He was pioneer as well as proprietor, and the scheme whose success brought him wealth originated rather in the poetic impulse to bring the beauty in which he himself delighted within the reach of thousands of lives (to be surely touched by contact with the glory of the West as with the refiner's fire), than in the masterly capacity for business which he brought to its working out. The kinship in the two natures soon showed itself, and they became daily companions. Mr. Hutcheson, whom his friends called the "Admiral of the West," and whom the Glaswegian pointed out as "the fallow that taks the shillins oot o' the watter," was a generous host, who welcomed to his steamers the whole commonwealth of art and letters. Poets and artists stepped on board with his visiting-card in hand, and the assurance that the officials understood to grant his guests an even finer courtesy than was assured to his passengers. This freedom of his fleet was soon extended to my father and to the members of his family. On the first day of May in every year that followed, until Mr. Hutcheson's failing health led him to withdraw from business, his card arrived, adding us to the host of his guests for the season. If my father delayed to come, a second would follow with a mandate or appeal, as suited the Admiral's humour. So for seven years our summer-home was at Oban, and that before the railway had found it out, or the hydropathic demon had alighted upon its wooded cliffs to blight them.

We were constant to an old-fashioned house which stood near the head of the main street of Oban, and commanded a view of its busiest portion. Beneath our windows flowed the stream of tourists to and from the steamers, and from them we could hail acquaintances on their arrival. The rooms were very popular, and were the scene of many a bright symposium. Indeed, my father's presence and that of Mr. Hutcheson attracted a sort of irregular and unceremonious *salon*, through which there passed " many men and many manners" indeed, but all with some gift of song or poem, adventure or anecdote, experience or wisdom, to enrich the hour of intercourse. The unfailing *habitués* were Mr. Hutcheson and Dr. M'Gillivray, the former a past-master at both song and story, the latter an ardent sportsman with rod and gun; while the touch Oban maintains with the South, which lures many a bird of passage to alight there a while, gave opportunity for sudden pleasant greetings and discoursings with poets, artists, men-of-letters, men of science, and sportsmen of every type. Such intercourse, free, desultory, full of surprises and variety, accorded with my father's nature, and refreshed him as the formal and calculated interchange of ordinary social life never attained to do. It was a compromise between the latter and the sylvan age to which he properly belonged, when a happy meeting between fauns and nymphs brought about a ball, and banquets were coincident with the laden vine-branch and the sparkling stream.

He fished a little in the neighbourhood of Oban, but without the energy and persistence of former years. Once he went to Mull, and paid Dr. Cumming a visit at Inellan, the little house on whose porch the inscription assures the coming guest of what it does not fail to give—" Parva domus, magna pax!" In Mull he fished a good deal, having received the Duke of Argyll's permission to do so. But while quartered in Oban, many of his days were spent on board the steamers, where his footing was both free and welcome, and where he was one of many a party to Staffa and Iona, to Glencoe or to Skye. He enjoyed the trip to Staffa most, and made it several times in each summer, always with some congenial companion, generally Mr. Hutcheson, and once, I remember, with ex-President Davies. The summer visit to Oban was the chief event of seven years—indeed until the death of most of his friends there made return painful, while his own increasing weakness prescribed change nearer home. Part of his enjoyment was contributed by the journey thither and back, in which he generally managed to include a visit to Mr. Glassford Bell in Glasgow. The Sheriff sometimes found his way to Oban for a few days, and one summer spent a whole month there with his wife and her sisters. It was the year before his death; and although he was exhausted by overwork, and by the first threatening of an illness which was soon to prove fatal, he was, as ever, fresh in spirit, and genially ready to enjoy what the day suggested. I remember particularly a picnic to Taynuilt in which we joined. My father had given me a fishing-rod and basket; and as the object of the excursion was to fish in the River Awe, I made bold to take them, supported by one of Mrs. Bell's sisters, who wished to fish and tie with me. When we reached Taynuilt, the two veteran anglers became aware of our presumption, and sternly interdicted us from the Awe, half contemptuously conceding to us a streamlet which finds its way into the river near the mouth. We unfurled our rod with meekness beside the humble tributary, and my father, relenting, came back to choose our flies and give us a lesson in casting. As the hours wore away, we caught a dozen trout between us, ending with scrupulous fairness when each had achieved her half-dozen. We were not elated, for the trout were small, and their collective weight was no great matter; and when we reached the rendezvous, we looked for glittering spoil of salmon and sea-trout worthy of our masters. A little flounder lay there, and that was all; and which of them had attained to catch it we never knew, for they were silent and eke sulky. When we emptied our creel, with some slight promptings of modest display, they shook with silent laughter, but forbore to praise us.

After leaving Oban in 1870, my father paid London a visit of some weeks, when I was his companion. The incident which gave him most pleasure on this occasion was an introduction to Dr. Frank Buckland, whom he visited several times at his work at South Kensington, and in whose collection and experiments he was naturally much interested. I remember, too, a visit to Richmond, when we sat for a long time by the Thames watching an old gentleman fishing from a punt. His arm-chair, umbrella, and placidity were all details of unwonted interest; and when, at the end of an hour, he caught a fish about as long as his finger, my father's excitement far exceeded his own. When that tribute to capture subsided, he roared with laughter.

From these brief wanderings, however much he enjoyed them, he returned to Kelso with satisfaction. On the morning that our faces were set homeward, whether from Oban or elsewhere, his was radiant; and as we reached the familiar neighbouring stations, his spirits overflowed in rhyme and pun and merry talk. We had a foolish lifelong jest about two imaginary friends, who had grown almost real to us from the ingenuity with which we had developed their characters and fortunes, and whose histories progressed at such moments. Sir William Jones, who had all gifts and graces, and Dr. Jones, his brother, who had gifts enough but little grace, were topics of such talk for more than thirty years, and became in the end so well defined that their materialisation would scarcely have surprised us.

When we reached Kelso in the evening, and were going by Maxwellheugh towards the bridge, he would triumphantly point out the beauty of the little town, with its touch of royal serenity, as in the Tweed's safe keeping, and defy the world to show him a fairer sight. And when, after the preliminary bustle, we shook ourselves into home-life again, and he had visited his roses and reported progress on his pears, and had gone to the reading-room to count cronies there, then indeed was he "shut up in measureless content."

In 1872 a great addition was made to his social resources when Mr. W. W. Tulloch, a son of Principal Tulloch's, came to assist, and eventually to succeed, the minister of the parish of Kelso. The young man and the old soon found each other out, and formed a friendship the interest of which was only accentuated by the difference in their years. The two were frequent companions in the daily walk by the river, and to Mr. Tulloch my father expressed fully and constantly his thoughts on " the things of the Spirit." A great humility and reverence were characteristic of his approach to these subjects, although he expressed with vigour his scorn of the makers of systems, who would silence the many voices which he felt to be of God in the heart of man. He cared to kneel directly at the throne as his right, but humbly as in the presence of the Almighty. The vast themes of God and Eternity were beyond man's limitation and verbal definition, but duty was clear enough ; and baring his head and looking up to the sky, he would repeat with the pathos of conviction, " He hath showed thee, O man, what is good : and what doth the Lord require of thee, but to do justly and to love mercy, and to walk humbly with thy God ? '

He criticised pretentious sermons with severity; and a friend, who knew and understood him, tells me that once, walking home from church, he said, "If I had my way, I would have a few of the best men in the Churches selected to write a series of fifty-two sermons for each year, and I would print one of these for each Sunday, and distribute it to be preached in all the churches in the country. In this way the whole body of the people would have the benefit of the ablest and best teachers in the land."

The pomp of worshippers excited his wrath, and he particularly disliked the carriages which dashed down the gravel walk from the Parish Church of Kelso, scattering the pedestrians to right and left. Once, when a menagerie was in the town, he announced his intention of hiring the elephant for Sunday use, and so scoring on the carriages. He thought that would keep them out of his way.

In 1874 my brother came home from New Zealand, accompanied by his wife, and they went with us to Oban. His keen angling fervour restimulated my father, and together they made a tour of the Highlands, dipping their rods in familiar streams. But the latter was no longer able for the fatigue of a prolonged fishing expedition, and was glad to return to Oban. Later in the season he made the acquaintance of Dr. Appleton, the original editor of the *Academy*. It was on board one of the West Highland steamers, on the occasion of its first summer trip to Skye. Mr. Hutcheson had invited about thirty of his friends to make the trip with him. Starting at six o'clock in the morning, we reached Loch Scavaig at noon, rested there a few hours, while we visited Loch Corruisk, and afterwards returned to Oban about ten o'clock at night. It was a perfect summer day, and the sea was astir with life, mackerel shoals, dolphins, sea-birds. Dr. Appleton, who was making a tour of the Highlands with his friend Mr. M'Lennan, was soon in touch with the "Admiral's" party, and was attracted by my father. During his short stay in

Oban he spent two evenings with us, while my father talked of the old days with Christopher North, the Shepherd, and De Quincey; and before he left he secured my father's promise to contribute reviews of angling literature to the *Academy*. This he did for the six following years. His successor on the staff of that journal is not, however, aware that his predecessor was an author of some repute on angling; for in a review, some years ago, of the literature of the "gentle craft," which starts from Juliana Berners, and embraces many a trivial publication of modern times, the "Angler's Companion" is conspicuous by its absence.

My father's attention was much occupied during the years between 1866 and 1876 by the strong interest, then becoming very general, in the preservation of the rivers and lochs of Scotland from pollution. Thanks to the work of the Tweed Commissioners, and of the Association organised at Edinburgh for informing and rousing public opinion on the subject, it had become a matter for serious consideration, which resulted in the Bill for the Prevention of the Pollution of Rivers, brought before the Houses of Parliament and made law in 1876. Up to that date, the rivers which had the misfortune to serve as drains for a series of towns, and which invited the neighbourhood of manufactories, were dulled and poisoned by the floods of refuse which they were doomed to receive. It is easy to imagine with what indignation my father viewed the growing evil—an indignation which found vent in letters, articles for the newspapers, and, as a matter of course, in poems. A few verses, of one of the last may be quoted, as suggestive of his wrath :—

> " River of all rivers dearest
>   To the Scottish heart—to ours !
> River without shade of rival,
>   Rolling crystals, nursing flowers ;
>
> " Stirring up the soul of music,
>   Chaunting, warbling, luting, chiming
> To the poet's ardent fancy,
>   Adept in the art of rhyming ;

"Marching onward through thy valley
  With the bearing of a king,
From the hundred hills surrounding
  All thy vassals summoning!

"Of our rivers still the glory!
  God defend it! there is need,
For the demon of pollution
  Campeth on the banks of Tweed.

"Pelf and Self! the double demon,
  From its clutch, good God, deliver!
Save from taint of the defiler,
  Saviour! save our dearest river!"

An experiment begun by a Special Committee of the Tweed Commissioners in the spring of 1874 also proved to have some interest for my father. On the 7th of May, a hundred and thirty-three smolts were taken from the Tweed while they were making their way to the sea, and were placed in a pond prepared for them on the Carham estate. They were declared to be the smolts of sea-trout by members of the Experimental Committee, fishermen, and *soi-disant* experts; but Major Dickins and my father were of opinion that they were the young of common trout. This opinion they maintained when the fish were examined two years after their confinement; and I believe they were dubbed " amateurs " for their pains. In May 1879, thirty of the fish were marked by a ring of silver wire, which was inserted behind the adipose fin, and were returned to the Tweed, where three of them were caught in the course of the summer. Two of these were brought to Mr. Brotherstone, the naturalist, who at once identified them as common trout, while the third was certified by the experienced fisher who caught it to be neither more nor less than another common trout. No one was less of an amateur or more exact in observation than my father, but these are not the attributes which give an opinion weight with theorists. Although he was undeniably angry with their obstinate misprision, he was still more amused by it, and on October 11th 1875, predicted their discomfiture in a long and able letter to the *Scotsman*.

In 1873 a collection of his later poems, under the title of "Songs of the Seasons," was published in Edinburgh by Messrs. Edmonston & Douglas. Besides the four poems which give it its main title, the book includes a number of songs, two ballads, some patriotic poems, a variety of musings on the problems of life and on passing events rendered in verse, and two addresses to his wife. Some stanzas of one of the last will illustrate the general character of its lyrical portion. They were written in anticipation of the yearly visit to Oban, and begin :—

> " In the heat of the year, ere June expires,
>   When the sun holds court in the Highlands high,
> And is lavish most of its marvel fires,
>   We'll off to Oban, you and I.

> " In the noon of the year, when the rage hath died
>   Out of the great Atlantic roll,
> And the spell is binding on wave and tide
>   That draws to Oban heart and soul ;

> " When Morven reveals its purpling heights,
>   And the banners of mist are all up-rolled ;

When the legion hath fled of sullen sprites,
    And the angel unravels his tissues of gold ;

" When over the maze of motley isles
    That ward our harbours from foe and storm,
The cloudland dissolves into wreaths of smiles,
    And the rainbow stretches its tremulous form ;

" When the blended breaths of the heath and thyme
    And balmy orchis are all astir ;
When in fairy ears the bluebells chime,
    And the cone is greening on the fir ;

" After the early life of the brae,
    The primrose joy and glory are past ;
After the honeymoon of the may,
    When its bridal attire the sloe hath cast ;

" After the merle hath ceased to sing,
    Or sings by starts in the gates of the eve ;
After the ' wandering voices of spring,'
    Cuckoo and curlew, have taken leave ;

" When the scowl is lifted from off the brows
    Of old Duntroon and grim Dunolly,
And there is the whisper of lovers' vows
    Below the hazels and the holly ;

"When the spectres that howl round Gylen stern
    In the winter nights are laid and at rest,
And the otter, gliding through cave and cairn
    In Kerrera fair, is its grimmest guest;

"In the heart of the year, when the salmon seek
    Their way to the rivers, and merry sea-trout
Give life by their frolics to bay and creek,
    When the lusty porpoise is rolling about;

"When the lythe is at play round the Eilan Dhu,
    And the dolorous gurnard shows on the calms,
And the hoe and stenlock dare and do
    The havoc of wolves among the lambs;

"When the crops of the sea are ripe and rife,
    Dainty and luring to palate and eye,
And its garners teem with the marvels of life—
    We'll off to Oban, you and I."

The old delight in Nature is fresh as ever in these verses, and the other poems in the volume are full of it; but in most of them some influence from the domain of prose has crept into its expression. The versified musings have an autobiographical interest. Probably the following lines contain the veriest commonplaces of modern philosophy;—their only value here is that they were part of the creed of a man who concerned himself in no wise about modern philosophy :—

> " Marry ! the past and its glories,
> Marry ! the past with its stories
> Of valour, and love, and ambition,
> Of tyranny, crime, and sedition,
> Of hope and despair, of joy and of sorrow,
> Foreshadows in its history
> The happenings of the morrow.
> Can we make more of the mystery ?
> One generation goeth,
> And lo ! another succeedeth,
> As o'er the billow that leadeth
> Another billow floweth.
>
> " The past in the future mergeth,
> And out of the future resurgeth !
> The present is but a tittle,
> Brave in its own esteem,
> But less than the veriest little—
> Of existence haply the dream !

> True! in our chrysalis state,
> We regard it as all in all;
> But in the scripture of fate,
> Conning the stars as we read,
> The present is thrown to the wall—
> Such is a leaf of our creed!"

The edition did not sell, although the book was favourably reviewed; and a number of the copies remained on the publishers' hands.

On September 27, 1876, the Kelso Angling Association presented my father with his portrait, in commemoration of his long connection with its members in both official and social relations.

His angling days were, however, nearly over. The four days weekly had dwindled down to one at the most, and gradually even that was often intermitted. His ailments were increasing, and frequent attacks of pain and nausea made it imprudent for him to incur the risk of chills and fatigue. When an interval of freedom from uneasiness encouraged him, he would take his rod and go up Teviot as of old; but he grew soon tired, and was apt to fall asleep on the bank.

Every day, morning and evening, in fine weather and bad, he went to the bridge to look at the Tweed. He had foretold these days in his youth, and now very literally fulfilled the foreboding :—

> "And I, when to breathe is a burden, and joy
> Forsakes me, and life is no longer the boy,
> On the labouring staff and the trem'rous knee
> Shall wander, bright river, to thee!"

During the last few years of his life he tried to fill the blank with gardening, and grew roses in the sunny little plot behind Bellevue Cottage with much success. I remember his pleasure when these rewarded his care, as well as his letters to me when I was from home urging me not to stay away beyond such and such a day, else I would miss some beautiful rose. When I came home, we went straight to the garden to look at his favourites, to count and admire them.

He managed to keep up a yearly visit to Yetholm Loch, which a friend, who was always of the party, describes as follows :—" Not the least part of Mr. Stoddart's enjoyment was in his preparations for the day, which generally took up the best part of the week beforehand. Trouts had to be caught to bait the pike-hooks, the tackle had to be carefully selected, worms had to be supplied for the perch, and a substantial luncheon for the party. Of all these the veteran angler claimed the charge, and well he did his work. On the morning he was generally the first ready. We met at Bellevue Cottage, got into our trap, and started in the full expectation of a happy day, which never failed to be realised. The drive to the loch lasted an hour, and he enlivened the way with his angling recollections, given with genuine humour—the Junction, the Quarry Hole, and Catch-a-penny all suggesting some bygone exploit. Arrived at Lochside House, we shoulder our equipments and march to the loch, where the boat lies ready for us. Rods are now put up and trimmed for the perch, floats are made ready, trouts attached to the pike-hooks by the master-hand, the luncheon-basket is not forgotten, and we embark, making the round of the loch before casting anchor, and then choosing the best taking spots. At the word of command our rods are all out, and we watch our corks, each eager to draw first blood. The bottom of the boat is soon covered with perch, but we do not wait to count our spoils until the shoal has passed us. Presently comes the welcome shout from Mr. Stoddart, ' We have him, and a monster too!' and turning to the bobbing float, we obey the order ' Up anchor and follow.' Left, right, left, right, we go, till we are on him. Time after time he eludes us; but at last Mr. Stoddart's practised hand has him in his toils, and soon Master Pike is drawn up, and goes floundering into the boat. We younger hands give the fresh-water shark a wide berth: not so our old friend. With the line in his hand, he gradually lifts the pike till it is almost at the perpendicular, then with a forked stick loosens the barbed hook from its throat, and plunges a sharp knife into its brain—when with a final spasm the monster dies. One float after another now begins to dance, and we have rare fun rushing hither and thither after our prey. The day wears on, and by and by we haul in our floats and count our prizes. We find seven pike, weighing from three to twelve pounds apiece, and over a hundredweight of perch to the four rods. We fought our battles over again as we drove home; and the annual excursion was for us all a red-letter day in the year."

The yearly visits to Yarrow had come to an end, but in summer my father and I generally made a day's excursion to St. Mary's Loch, taking an early train to Selkirk and the "Flower of Yarrow" coach up the valley to the old haunt. One year, as we drove past a broom-clad bank near the Yarrow Feus, the blaze of yellow blossom was so impressive that it set fire to his fancy, and he quickly conceived a Romaunt of Yarrow, which should tell how broom from Cowdenknowes was brought by wizard's spell to Yarrow. He began to turn his fantastic tale into verse, and chose the old Scots tongue for his medium, a language he understood well in the finer dialect which our ancestors used, which is now extinct. The chief figure in the story was meant to be the wizard of Balwearie, Michael Scot; but the plot was not well contrived, and the adventures of subordinate characters detract from the main interest of a rhymed romance which was never finished, and whose fragment leaves a confused impression upon the reader.

He was busy with this when Messrs. J. & J. H. Rutherfurd of Kelso took over the copies of "Songs of the Seasons" which remained on the hands of the Edinburgh publishers, and asked him to write a short autobiography with which to preface their issue. This he was willing to do; but illness and long periods of prostration made the work very desultory, and it contains besides one regrettable passage, in which he accuses an old and valued friend by name of an unjust allegation of which he was not the source. The autobiography was his latest literary labour. The pen outlasted the rod. In June 1879, while fishing in Teviot some miles above Kelso, he fell into the Turn Pool, where the water is deep and rushing; and, although he was able to extricate himself without help, it was with the greatest difficulty that he got home. The incident warned him that the infirmities of age were upon him, and that he must not again risk such an adventure. In addition to his other ailments he suffered much from cramp, and every chill increased his pain and weakness. One last success awaited him. In September of the same year Mr. Thistlethwayte had taken the Tweed fishing between the Junction and Sharpitlaw Mill, but was unable to come to it for some weeks. He gave Mr. Forrest the freedom of his stretch of river for himself and his friends. Mr. Forrest met my father one fine fishing-day, and tempted him down to the boat. He was so frail that he could only hold his rod for ten minutes at a time; but when, below the cauld, he hooked a fish, the old familiar shock braced him up, and he played the salmon and landed it with all his wonted delicacy and certainty. He was not able to carry his prize home, however—although it did not weigh more than eight pounds; but Mr. Forrest took that trouble for him, and saw him safely to Bellevue Cottage. He was much pleased, but never fished again. During the summer of that year he went to Spittal for change of air; but received little benefit from his stay, and returned to Kelso glad to be at home.

The winter passed as usual—his days divided by short walks, his evenings spent at home, occupied with his "Autobiography" and "A Romaunt of Yarrow." The attacks of pain and nausea continued; but lasted a short time, and seldom interfered with his daily routine.

The summer of 1880 was a trying one for him. Suffering much from sleeplessness and loss of appetite, he tried sea-air once more at Spittal, but quickly returned worse than when he went. He revived a little in the quiet of home; but the intervals of freedom from discomfort were short and less frequent. On August 10th he wrote: "I have been walking in the Valley of the Shadow of Death; no sleep, little appetite, constant nausea. Thank God, my mind is entire, and I am able to divide my attention between the garden and my desk. That my hours are numbered I know, and am engaged in setting my house in order and making my peace with God. Come early in September—the 1st, if possible. I hope to have plenty of roses in blossom, carnations, and fuchsias."

Later in the month he wrote a little more cheerfully; and when I reached Kelso on the 4th of September, I found him awaiting me at the station, looking frail, but better than I had expected. A favourite niece came to stay with us, and her presence helped to brighten up the following weeks—although from time to time he suffered from the now wonted attacks of pain and depression.

Early in November he seemed sufficiently well to make it possible for me to pay a visit which was long due to some friends in Leyden.

My cousin and I left home for London—my father seeing us off at the Kelso station, bidding us farewell with a return of his old sunny humour. His last words to us were a jest about "Dr Jones," with whom my cousin had grown well acquainted during her stay.

He had given me a commission to bring him a box full of bulbs from Holland, and the letters which I received from him while at Leyden were occupied with his wishes respecting them. The last, written on the 18th of November, ended with the words, "Weary, weary, weary, is now the song of my life."

He posted that letter, and then walked feebly to the bridge to look at the Tweed. On his return home he felt very ill, and desired to go to bed and see his doctor. At first it was supposed that he suffered from a worse attack than usual, but that he would recover as usual. It was, however, soon recognised that this was the end; and shortly after receiving his letter, I was summoned home by telegram. I reached

Bellevue Cottage on Sunday the 21st, to find him unconscious; and, at four o'clock on Monday morning, he passed into the painless life with a gentle sigh. He sleeps in the Kelso Cemetery, in a spot chosen some months before his death by himself, "where I can hear the Tweed," he said;—and five years later, the wife whom he had wooed with love so sudden and yet so true half a century before, was laid beside him.

ELEGY

ON THE LATE

THOMAS TOD STODDART,

By Sir George Douglas, Bart.

By Tweed, by Teviot's winding tide,
    A form I knew is miss'd to-day!
The woods, the field, the rocks abide,
    But he has pass'd away—

Where, pensive—straying without an aim—
    As now, once more, these paths I trace
(Familiar haunts found still the same),
    I seek him in his place!

For seldom—(whether Tweed ran strong,
    Discoloured, swoll'n with melting snows,
Awful with wrecks it bears along
    'Twixt banks it overflows;

Whether, with summer-shrunken stream—
    Where isles, before unknown, appear—
It sank in sloth, resign'd to dream)—
    I failed to meet him here!

Indeed—by drought, fair skies, or flood—
    So constant this his walk had been,
He seemed, when met in fancy's mood,
    The Genius of the scene.

Or, even—with venerable beard;
    In his right hand a willow-rod—
Late sighted where his name was fear'd
    The very river-god!

His date was from that Golden Age
    When, sprung from Hercules and Mirth,
In manhood and poetic rage,
    Giants still dwelt on earth.

In mountain, water, field, and wood,
    Their might was felt—empowered, at will,
The broods of earth, the sky, the flood,
    To capture, tame, or kill.

Then, by the fair lake's margent clear,
    What nights were theirs! how brave a feast!
Ranged all in order, peer by peer,
    Where he was not the least.

Methinks the moon was full by night,
    When Madness, madder than before,
Drank deep, and kept till broad daylight
    That table in a roar!

But envying Time, with marksman's art,
    Waging dire war, slew, one by one,
Their race large-limb'd and light of heart—
    Till he remained alone:

And lingering, lonely, very old,
    Saw baser times, and knew instead
Men in whose veins the blood ran cold,
    With hearts where mirth was dead.

Yet still his peaceful craft he plied,
    Haunting by river, lake, and rill—
With power to common men denied,
    Assiduous, angling still.

Till all in wonderment cried out,
    When he, at eve, his ploy forsook—
From head to heel, and round about,
    Hung with the spoils he took!

He dipt his fingers in the flood
    (I heard an ancient angler tell),
And, nibbling, straight the finny brood
    Swarm'd at the charmer's spell.

And sometimes, too, with childlike glee,
    In praise of stream and river-side,
He sang. A kindly man was he;
    And so, in time, he died.

And thus, by Teviot's rolling flood,
    His well-known form we miss to-day—
Gazing on river, field, and wood,
    Whence he has passed away!

Dear poet! from that dead hand of thine,
    I (oh! not rashly) born too late,
Claiming far kinship in the line,
    This legacy await:—

To others other gifts: to me,
    If I have praised thee here, at last,
Though ill, not unacceptably,
    Thy poet's pipe be pass'd!

Now, sleep ! Thy songs thou leavest with us :
   Thy story be it our task to tell ;
But thee, we now departing, thus,
   Salute and bid "Farewell!"

ANGLING SONGS.

ANGLING SONGS.

THE ANGLER'S VINDICATION.

I.

Say not our hands are cruel,
    What deeds invite the blame?
Content our golden jewel,
    No blemish on our name:
        Creation's lords
        We need no swords
To win a withering fame.

II.

Say not in gore and guile
    We waste the livelong day:
Let those alone revile
    Who feel our subtile sway,

When fancy-led
The sward we tread
And while the morn away.

III.

Oh! not in camp or court
   Our best delights we find,
But in the far resort
   With water, wood, and wind,
     Where Nature works
     And beauty lurks
In all her craft enshrined.

IV.

There captive to her will,
   Yet 'mid our fetters free,
We seek by singing rill
   The broad and shady tree,
     And lisp our lay
     To flower and fay,
Or mock the linnet's glee.

v.

Thus glides the golden hour,
　　Until the chimes to toil
Recall from brook and bower;
　Then, laden with our spoil,
　　　Slowly we part
　　　With heavy heart
　And leave the haunted soil.

TROLLING SONG.

I.

The bell-throats o' the bonny birds ring,
    When the angler goes a-trolling;
The south wind waves his cheery wing,
    And gentle rains are falling.

II.

The white thorn bears its bridal wreath,
    When the angler goes a-trolling;
And hark! along the bloomy heath
    The plaintive plover calling!

III.

Breezy and brown the rivers glide,
    When the angler goes a-trolling;
The dark burns leave the green hill-side
    Among the pebbles brawling.

IV.

Upon the meadow, by the springs,
    The quiet herds are lolling;
All earth is full of happy things
    When the angler goes a-trolling!

THE ANGLER'S COMPLAINT.

I.

THEY'VE steekit the waters agen us, Jock,
    They've steekit the burnies an' a';
We hae na a chiel to befrien' us, Jock,
    Our laird's aye makin' the law.

II.

We'll get neither yallow nor grey-fin, Jock,
    Nor bull-heid nor sawmon ava;
The laird he's aye at the savin', Jock,
    An' hauds to us weel wi' his law.

III.

Yer flees ye may set them a bleezin', Jock,
    Our wands they may gang to the wa';
It's neither in rhyme nor in reason, Jock,
    To coort a kick-up wi' the law.

IV.

That ilka intent should miscarry, Jock,
    I dinna wunner ava;
Our laird he's kin to the Shirra, Jock,
    And sib wi' the loons o' the law.

V.

But faith! ye'll agree it's a hardship, Jock,
    To gie up our richts to the craw;
The neist time we meet wi' his lairdship, Jock,
    We promise him licks for his law.

VI.

An' e'en when the mirk is a-nearin', Jock,
    Wi' pock-nets and drag-nets an' a',
We'll gie his bit ponds sic a clearin', Jock,
    Our laird he'll look twice to the law.

VII.

We'll no spare a ged or a gudgeon, Jock,
    We'll no spare a fin or a jaw;
Lord pity the crazy curmudgeon, Jock!
    He'll sune tak his leave o' the law!

TO THE NAIRN.

I.

WATER of Alders! where is the spell
    That binds me in spirit to thee?
I cared not to drop my farewell,
For I left no loved things, in meadow or dell,
    Thou wert but a stranger with me.

II.

Yet, in my fancy, often I turn
    From the streams of my choice, all apart—
From the sylvan and blossomy burn
To the vale where thy waters murmur and mourn,
    Their memory hangs on the heart!

III.

Often in vision tempt me again
    Thy wild roving shoals; but I bend

O'er the silent shapes of the slain,
Not for me from the depths of the billowy main
   The living thy channels ascend.

IV.

Swift as an arrow glancing below
   Speeds the silver trout of the sea,
And ever on thy autumnal flow
The salmon laving his bosom of snow
   Wends hill-ward, but not for me!

V.

Water of Alders! memory brings
   Me back to each trodden fane,
And its silent recall of banished things
Unfetters Affection's buried springs
   And bids them gush forth again!

SONG.

I.

When homeward from the stream we turn
    Good cheer our sport replaces,
There's liquor twinkling in the glass,
    There's joy on all our faces!

II.

We drink sweet healths, a merry round,
    We talk old stories over,
And sing glad staves, like summer birds
    Below their leafy cover.

III.

Thus cheerily our evenings pass,
    Till lulled below the quilting
We sleep our toils off, and are forth
    Before the lark is lilting.

SONG.

IV.

All joy be with our hearts' kin bold!
   May care's nets ne'er entangle,
Nor woe nor poverty depress
   A brother of the angle!

THE HOLY-WELL POOL.

I.

When the month is happy June,
And her horns forsake the moon—
When she greets us round and full,
Then we'll haunt the Holy-well pool.
 Where I ween,
 'Neath willow green,
Bright fins are ever gliding;
 'Mong the reeds
 And water-weeds,
They hold their wary hiding.

II.

Not by moonlight need we tread
Mossy bank or river-bed;
No living things 'neath moonlight prowl,
Save beetle and bat and solemn owl;

THE HOLY-WELL POOL.

  As she rides
  The old trout hides,
Under the still bank deeper;
  Nor sweet fly
  Nor minnow sly
Can rouse the silent sleeper.

III.

Rather at morn-tide we shall go
To the Holy-well when the sun is low,
Ere the bee visits the new-burst flower
Or the noon breeze shakes the bower;
  Then the trout
  Sails round about
Beyond the osier bushes,
  Or descries
  His winged prize
Among the whispering rushes.

IV.

Then we'll seek the Holy-well,
Or when eve glides up the dell,

And the cushat all unseen
Coos among the larch-wood green
 Stealing soft
 Along the croft
We'll beat the shady water,
 Till to rest
 With arm opprest
Night turns us from the slaughter.

MUSINGS.

I.

Welcome, sweet southern showers!
Welcome, ye early flowers,
   Woo'd by the bee!
Ever gentle and bland
To all wights of the wand
   Welcome are ye!

II.

Oft at the wintry fire,
Nursing our hearts' desire
   Fondly we dream
Of joy in the breeze—
Singing birds on the trees—
   Flowers by the stream.

III.

Often our fancy brings
Pictures of sunny things
　　Home to our hearth,
And we seem as we stray'd
Among sunshine and shade,
　　Music and mirth.

IV.

Then with unconscious hand
Grasp we the idle wand,
　　Full of the boy,
When to our sad surprise
Swiftly the vision flies,
　　Summer and joy!

SONNET.—CONAN FALLS.

Through Luichart's lone expanse dark Conan flows,
Of moorland nature, as its tawny blood
Betokens, and insensibly the flood
Glides onward, while continuous hills enclose
The quiet lake ; at length, this soft repose—
The Syren bosom of the pastoral deeps
It rudely spurns, and with terrific leaps
Descends into the valley.   Oft I chose
In days by-gone the wild and wizard place
Wherein to roam, and from the eddy's rout
Lured with bewitching fly the wary trout ;
This scene hath Time's hand shifted, and its face
'Reft of the life ; yet, picture-like, to me
It hangs within the Mind's dark gallery.

THE TAKING OF THE SALMON.

I.

A BIRR! a whirr! a salmon's on,
   A goodly fish! a thumper!
Bring up, bring up the ready gaff,
And if we land him we shall quaff
   Another glorious bumper!
   Hark! 'tis the music of the reel,
     The strong, the quick, the steady;
   The line darts from the active wheel,
     Have all things right and ready.

II.

A birr! a whirr! the salmon's out,
   Far on the rushing river;
Onward he holds with sudden leap,
Or plunges through the whirlpool deep,
   A desperate endeavour!

Hark to the music of the reel!
    The fitful and the grating;
It pants along the breathless wheel,
    Now hurried—now abating.

III.

A birr! a whirr! the salmon's off!—
    No, no, we still have got him;
The wily fish is sullen grown,
And, like a bright imbedded stone,
    Lies gleaming at the bottom.
Hark to the music of the reel!
    'Tis hushed, it hath forsaken;
With care we'll guard the magic wheel,
    Until its notes rewaken.

IV.

A birr! a whirr! the salmon's up,
    Give line, give line and measure;
But now he turns! keep down ahead,
And lead him as a child is led,
    And land him at your leisure.

Hark to the music of the reel!
    'Tis welcome, it is glorious;
It wanders through the winding wheel,
    Returning and victorious.

V.

A birr! a whirr! the salmon's in,
    Upon the bank extended;
The princely fish is gasping slow,
His brilliant colours come and go,
    All beautifully blended.
    Hark to the music of the reel!
        It murmurs and it closes;
    Silence is on the conquering wheel,
        Its wearied line reposes.

VI.

No birr! no whirr! the salmon's ours,
    The noble fish—the thumper:
Strike through his gill the ready gaff,
And bending homewards, we shall quaff
    Another glorious bumper!

Hark to the music of the reel !
    We listen with devotion ;
There's something in that circling wheel
    That wakes the heart's emotion !

SEEK YE WHAR THE BURNIE TRAVELS.

I.

Seek ye whar the burnie travels,
    Sullied wi' the simmer showers,
Whar the fairy hauds his revels
    In the cleuch amang the flowers?
      Seek ye there, free o' care
      To dip the flowin' line,
    Wi' skilfu' hand to wave the wand
      An' dip the flowin' line!

II.

Or mayhap, whar glen desertin'
    Winds the river blue and braid;
Noo some quiet meadow skirtin',
    Rinnin' noo anent the shade;
      Seek ye there, &c.

III.

Or amang the hills uncheery
   Whar the mirk mere slumbers lorn,
An' his dirges lang and dreary
   Pipes the grey whaup to the morn.
     Seek ye there, &c.

THE VOICE OF THE CUCKOO.

I.

Is the cuckoo come? Is the cuckoo come?
  Seek ye its happy voice
  Bidding the hills rejoice,
Greeting green summer and sweet May morn?
  See you the bird,
  Or hear its loved word
From dewy birch-wood or aged thorn?

II.

Is the cuckoo come? Is the cuckoo come?
  Down by the reedy spring
  Watching its wary wing
Wends the lone angler toward the lake,
  Joy in his heart
  With fancy alert,
He rears gentle visions wandering awake.

III.

Is the cuckoo come? Is the cuckoo come?
 Lover of sunny streams!
 Banish thy airy dreams,
Hark the wild note of the fairy-voiced bird!
 Now in the glen,
 And listen again,
O'er the wide hill floats the silvery word.

IV.

Is the cuckoo come? Is the cuckoo come?
 Haste to thy loved resort,
 Haste to thy pleasant sport,
Shake the sly palmer o'er streamlet and lake!
 Hark on the wind—
 Before thee—behind—
Plaintively singeth the bird of the brake!

O WAKEN, WINDS, WAKEN!

I.

O WAKEN, winds, waken! the waters are still,
And silence and sunlight recline on the hill;
The angler is watching beside the green springs
For the low welcome sound of your wandering wings!

II.

His rod is unwielded, his tackle unfreed,
And the withe-woven pannier lies flung on the mead;
He looks to the lake, through its fane of green trees,
And sighs for the curl of the cool summer breeze.

III.

Calm-bound is the form of the water-bird fair,
And the spear of the rush stands erect in the air,
And the dragon-fly roams o'er the lily-bed gay,
Where basks the bold pike in a sun-smitten bay.

IV.

O waken, winds, waken ! wherever asleep,
On cloud or dark mountain, or down in the deep;
The angler is watching, beside the green springs,
For the low welcome sound of your wandering wings.

SONNET.—THE ETTRICK SHEPHERD.

THE fellow-anglers of my youthful days,
(Of past realities we form our dream,)
I watch them re-assembling by the stream,
And on the group with solemn musings gaze ;
For some are lost in life's bewildering haze,
And some have left their sport and tak'n to toil,
And some have faced the Ocean's wild turmoil,
And some—a very few—their olden ways
By shining lake and river still pursue ;
Ah ! *one* I gaze on 'mid the fancied band,
Unlike the rest in years, in gait, in hue—
Uprisen from a dim and shadowy land—
Ask what loved phantom fixes my regard !
Yarrow's late pride, the Angler, Shepherd, Bard !

THE RIVER.

I.

THROUGH sun-bright lakes,
   Round islets gay,
The river takes
   Its western way,
And the water-chime
Soft zephyrs time
   Each gladsome summer day.

II.

The starry trout,
   Fair to behold,
Roameth about
   On fin of gold;
At root of tree
His haunt you may see,
   Rude rock or crevice old.

III.

And hither dart
  The salmon grey,
From the deep heart
  Of some sea bay;
And herling wild
Is here beguiled
  To hold autumnal play.

IV.

Oh! 'tis a stream
  Most fair to see,
As in a dream
  Flows pleasantly;
And our hearts are woo'd
To a kind sweet mood
  By its wondrous witchery.

TROLLING SONG.

I.

Let us go a trolling, boys!
A trolling we shall go,
While the showers are falling, boys,
And while the south winds blow;
Where the trout
Prowl about,
Steadily, steadily, let us row.

II.

See! the waves are dancing, boys,
Around the mermaid isle;
Many a fin is glancing, boys,
Oh! weary runs the while,
Till we speed,
All agreed
To troll, to troll the glittering guile.

III.

O'er the surface ranging, boys,
    We'll beat from bay to bay,
Lure and water changing, boys;
    It is the angler's way;
        So we'll troll
        One and all
And cheerily, cheerily pass the day.

IV.

And again returning, boys,
    We'll talk our triumphs o'er,
Tongue and bosom burning, boys,
    As they have burned before,
        While we told
        Feats of old,
We never, we never can equal more!

THE SEA-TROUT GREY.

I.

The sea-trout grey
Are now at play,
The salmon is up, hurra! hurra!
For the streamlets brown
Are dancing down,
So quicken the cup, hurra! hurra!

II.

The cloud-cap still
Is on the hill,
And the showers fall fast, hurra! hurra!
But the sun and breeze
Will scatter these,
So drink while they last, hurra! hurra!

III.

We'll start by dawn
O'er lea and lawn,
Through thicket and thorn, hurra! hurra!
On merriest limb
With rods in trim,
Come drink a sweet morn, hurra! hurra!

AN ANGLER'S RAMBLES.

I.

I'VE angled far and angled wide,
On Fannich drear, by Luichart's side,
    Across dark Conan's current;
Have haunted Beauly's silver stream,
Where glimmering thro' the forest Dream
    Hangs its eternal torrent;

II.

Among the rocks of wild Maree,
O'er whose blue billow ever free
    The daring eagles hover,
And where, at Glomach's ruffian steep,
The dark stream holds its angered leap,
    Many a fathom over;

III.

By Lochy sad, and Laggan lake,
Where Spey uncoils his glittering snake
    Among the hills of thunder;
And I have swept my fatal fly
Where swarthy Findhorn hurries by
    The olden forest under:

IV.

On Tummel's solitary bed,
And where wild Tilt and Garry wed
    In Athol's heathery valleys,
On Earn by green Duneira's bower,
Below Breadalbane's Tay-washed tower,
    And Scone's once regal palace.

V.

There have I swept the slender line,
And where the broad Awe braves the brine,
    Have watched the grey grilse gambol,

By nameless stream and tarn remote,
With light flies in the breeze afloat,
    Holding my careless ramble.

VI.

But dearer than all these to me
Is sylvan Tweed; each tower and tree
    That in its vale rejoices!
Dearer the streamlets one and all,
That blend with its Eolian brawl
    Their own enamouring voices!

DRINKING SONG.

I.

While others are brawling let anglers agree,
    And in concord the goblet replenish;
Should contention prevail, then away on the gale
    All mirth and hilarity vanish.

II.

No strife we'll allow, no clamorous words
    To sever the friendships of summer,
But hand within hand, in amity stand,
    And consign every wrong to the rummer.

III.

Oh! Peace and Content are the angler's best wealth,
    No journey without them he ventures;
Like angels they wait at the porch of his gate,
    And greet him again when he enters.

IV.

Then joyously mingle the soul of the grain
    With a merry supply from the tankard!
"Twill cost not a care, as long as we share
    The cups of content and of concord!

THE YELLOW FINS O' YARROW.

I.

The yellow fins o' Yarrow dale!
　I kenna whar they've gane tae;
Were ever troots in Border vale
　Sae comely or sae dainty?

II.

They had baith gowd and spanglit rings,
　Wi' walth o' pearl amang them;
An' for sweet luve o' the bonny things,
　The heart was laith to wrang them.

III.

But he that angles Yarrow ower,
　(Maun changes ever waken?)
Frae our Lady's Loch to Newark Tower,
　Will find the stream forsaken.

IV.

Forsaken ilka bank an' stane
    O' a' its troots o' splendour;
Auld Yarrow's left sae lorn and lane,
    Ane scarcely wad hae kenn'd her.

V.

Waes me! the auncient yellow fin
    I marvel whar he's gane tae;
Was ever troot in Forest rin
    Sae comely or sae dainty!

A PICTURE.

We listen by the waters blue to voices that we love;
Sweet flowers are twinkling at our side, and willow leaves above;
Before us feeds the fearless trout, emerging from the calm,
And bleats behind the fleecy ewe upon its wandering lamb.

Delicious musings fill the heart, and images of bliss;
Ah! that all pictures of the past were innocent as this,—
That life were like a summer trance beneath a willow wide,
Or the ramble of an angler lone along the river-side.

A PECK O' TROUBLES.

I.

Gie me my gaud, my guid auld gaud—
　The wan' I lo'e sae rarely;
But faith, guidwife, it's unco thraw'd,
　Ye hae na used it fairly.

II.

The bairns! plague tak the thievin' things!
　They play the verra deevil;
Wha'd think they've hashed my lav'rock wings,
　An' ta'en my mennin sweevil?

III.

They've made sair wark amang the flees,
　There's neither huik nor hackle;
What's a' the guid o' brew or breeze
　An' no ane skein o' tackle?

IV.

But, hinny, whar's my muckle reel?
    Gie up yer cloots and needle—
I wadna lose my honest wheel
    For a' the wives in Tweeddale.

V.

No to the fore ! I micht hae guess'd
    Some ill or ither cam o't;
It's gane the gate o' a' the rest,
    An' nane to bear the blame o't.

VI.

Aweel ! aweel ! mishaps we ken
    Are coupled aye thegither ;
But, guidwife, rax us yonner hen,
    She's dainty in the feather.

VII.

A mawkin lug and tinsey braw,
    Ben in the kist ye'll find them,

Auld reel and tippets—airns an' a'—
  The airns, be shure an' mind them!

VIII.

It gangs awee agen the grain
  To bear sae mony troubles;
An' yet, guidwife, to ilka ane
  There's graith amang the stubbles.

IX.

It's neither dole nor deep lament
  Will mend a body's grievance;
Sae e'en we'll haud oursels content
  Wi' thae wee bits o' leevins;

X.

An' gin a sawmon soom the Tweed
  (The thing's no that unchancy,)
We'll gar the ilka tooth o't bleed,
  May fortune fa' the fancy!

THE ANGLER'S BENEDICTION.

I.

Bless with me the spring-tide bland,
　All ye anglers of the valley!
Wave aloof the slender wand,
　And around the oak-tree rally.

II.

Bless the birds, that all along
　Send us such a cheerful greeting;
To their measures of kind song
　Joyously our hearts are beating.

III.

Fleeted now the winter snow
　From the forehead of the mountains,
And the wild sweet waters flow
　Freshly through their several fountains.

IV.

In the secret of the sod,
    Moss and primrose lie together;
But the wild bee shoots abroad,
    Fonder of the April heather.

V.

Fresh and free the breezes blow,
    And the amber stream runs gaily;
Forth, and warble as ye go,
    All ye anglers of the valley!

SONNET.—THE RIVER EDEN.

Thomson! this quiet stream the song of thought
Oft in thy bosom reared, and as I steal
Along its banks, they to my gaze reveal
The pictures by thy truthful pencil wrought;
No rash intruder on the rural spot
I seem, but in that glowing fervour share,
Which on their page thy far-fam'd "Seasons" bear;
Nor honoured less is Nature, nor less sought
Her still retreats, while with my wand I fling
O'er Eden's pools the well-dissembling fly,
Creating in the Mind's fantastic eye
Castles of Indolence. The sudden spring
Of a huge trout assails their air-built walls,
And to the untrench'd earth each hollow fabric falls.

WHEN THE STREAMS RISE.

I.

When the streams rise,
When the wind flies,
With hope and delight we grow dizzy,
And all a-near
Airy words hear,
Be busy, sweet angler, be busy!

II.

Then we prepare
Tackle and hair,
And levy fair minnows full plenty,
Or armed with hoe
A-gathering go
Of brandlings and dew-feeders dainty.

III.

Then from the spring
Mosses we bring
To store our fresh baits before starting,
Young and unshorn,
Green in the horn,
Culled when the clouds are departing.

IV.

Thus duly stored,
Cunning or froward
No fish can say nay to our tackle,
While each we ply,
Worm, penk and fly,
Grey palmer or liveried hackle.

V.

Heigh for a wind
Gushing behind!
Heigh for a cloud dark and showery!

Foamy and freed,
Let the stream speed
Under the willow bough flowery

VI.

So may we start,
Joyous in heart,
With hope and felicity dizzy,
And still a-near
Airy words hear,
Be busy, sweet angler, be busy!

SONG.

I.

Bring the rod, the line, the reel!
Bring, oh bring the osier creel!
Bring me flies of fifty kinds,
Bring me showers, and clouds, and winds!
   All things right and tight,
      All things well and proper,
   Trailer red and bright,
      Dark and wily dropper—
Casts of midges bring,
      Made of plover-hackle,
With a gaudy wing,
      And a cobweb tackle.

II.

Lead me where the river flows,
Show me where the alder grows,
Reeds and rushes, moss and mead,
To them lead me—quickly lead,

Where the roving trout
    Watches round an eddy,
With his eager snout
    Pointed up and ready,
Till a careless fly
    On the surface wheeling,
Tempts him rising sly
    From his safe concealing.

III.

There, as with a pleasant friend,
I the happy hours will spend
Urging on the subtle hook,
O'er the dark and chancy nook,
    With a hand expert
        Every motion swaying,
    And on the alert
        When the trout are playing;
Bring me rod and reel,
    Flies of every feather,
Bring the osier creel—
    Send me glorious weather!

THE FLEE.

I.

Awa' wi' yer tinsey sae braw!
Our troots winna thole it ava,
   They've grown sae capricious,
   Sonsie and vicious—
As weel may ye fish wi' a craw.

II.

The wits o' an eel I'll uphaud
Agen baith the gowk and his gaud,
   Wha bounces and blethers
   O' fancies and feathers,
Till the lugs o' the lieges are staw'd.

III.

Wee dour-lookin' huiks are the thing,
Moose body an' laverock wing;
   There's mony a chiel ta'en ane
   Wi' mauk or wi' mennin,
But the flee answers best in the spring.

THE ANGLER'S TRYSTING-TREE.

I.

Sing, sweet thrushes, forth and sing!
    Meet the morn upon the lea;
Are the emeralds of spring
    On the angler's trysting-tree?
Tell, sweet thrushes, tell to me,
    Are there buds on our willow-tree?
    Buds and birds on the trysting-tree?

II.

Sing, sweet thrushes, forth and sing!
    Have you met the honey-bee,
Circling upon rapid wing
    Round the angler's trysting-tree?
Up, sweet thrushes, up and see;
    Are there bees at our willow-tree?
    Birds and bees at the trysting-tree?

III.

Sing, sweet thrushes, forth and sing!
    Are the fountains gushing free?
Is the south wind wandering
    Through the angler's trysting-tree?
Up, sweet thrushes, tell to me,
Is the wind at our willow-tree?
Wind or calm at the trysting-tree?

IV.

Sing, sweet thrushes, up and sing!
    Wile us with a merry glee,
To the flowery haunts of spring—
    To the angler's trysting-tree.
Tell, sweet thrushes, tell to me,
Are there flowers 'neath our willow-tree?
Spring and flowers at the trysting-tree?

THE LAIRD'S CAST.

I.

Fast! fast! we have him fast,
　　A prime one by the gleam!
In the old Laird's shadowy cast
　　Above the Elshie stream;
'Tis a salmon plump and strong,
　　Newly run from the distant brine,
Newly run, newly run,—a right thundering one!
　　Tell him line.

II.

Away, he darts away,
　　Across the shining Tweed,
Nor art nor arm can stay
　　The noble creature's speed;
From our reel the swift line spins,
　　As he feels the galling scar,
And in vain, all in vain, shakes his lengthening chain
　　From afar.

III.

To shore, slow draw to shore ;
    The light boat edges in,
While moves the cautious oar,
    Like some sea-prowler's fin
In the creeks of an Indian isle ;
    Now the flowery bank we've gained,
And in hand, firm in hand, with our labouring wand,
    Hold him chained.

IV.

See, see, in wild despair,
    He seeks by fatal spring
To break the magic hair—
    To fly the madd'ning string ;
In vain, all in vain, his headlong plunge !
    For the fatal die is cast ;
O'er his eyelid soon death's glimmering swoon
    Gathers fast.

V.

With quick revolving hand
    The good line home we wind,
While obedient to our wand
    The worn fish floats behind,
And the bright pebbled edge as he nears,
    With our gaff-hook we check his retreat,
And see, here he lies, a weltering prize
        At our feet!

SONNET.

"ANGLERS! ye are a heartless bloody race,"
'Tis thus the half-soul'd sentimentalist
Presumes to apostrophise us to the face;
Weak, paltry, miserable antagonist!
To deem by this compassionate grimace
He doth sweet service to humanity;
And yet when of his fellows' misery,—
Of wars, of pestilence, and the woes that chase
Mankind to the interminable shore
He hears, to treat them with a hasty sneer,
Nor let their shrill appeal disturb a tear
Or one emotion waken in his core!
It is too much! Anglers, your cruelty
Is tend'rer than this man's philanthropy.

THE GENTLE CRAFT.

I.

A JOLLY craft have we, hurra!
    The brethren of the streams!
In joy we pass the welcome day,
    And close it under dreams.
We wander by the river-side
    And by the gentle rill!
They roll along the valley wide—
    They gambol on the hill.

II.

It is a manly one and free,
    This pleasant sport of ours;
Above us is the shady tree
    And under us the flowers;

And in our hand the pliant rod
    Is waving to and fro—
The salmon lies upon the sod,
    Glittering like the snow.

III.

We love the angler's quiet lot,
    His meditative art;
The fancies in his hour of thought
    That blossom from his heart.
All other things we'll cast behind,
    Let busy toil alone,
And flinging care unto the wind,
    We'll angle, angle on.

YE WARDERS OF THE WATERS.

I.

Ye warders of the waters!
　Is the alder'd stream-side free?
　　Hath the salmon sped
　　From his winter bed
　Adown to the azure sea?
　　Rideth afloat
　　The fisher's boat
　Below the white-thorn tree?

II.

Go forth, ye anglers jovial!
　The waters are open wide;
　　No longer we ward
　　From vernal sward
　The glittering salmon glide;

Free at your will
The crystal rill,
And tuneless torrent-side.

III.

Ho! warders of the waters!
Is the yellow trout at feed?
And the March flies brown
Are they sailing down
Where current and zephyr lead?
See you abroad
With pliant rod
Some gentle brother speed?

IV.

Go forth, ye anglers, jovial!
The ring of the trout we spy,
And the south winds pour
In a pleasant shower
The merry March-brown fly;
With vigorous wand
The fisher band
Among the dark pools ply.

THE ANGLER'S JOYS.

I.

Oh! who that feels the joyous throb, which the angler's bosom stirreth,
    To the flowery stream-side hieing,
    When vernal winds are flying,
Would envy all that Fortune with her fickle hand conferreth?

II.

Nor in cities, nor with courtiers, nor within the kingly palace,
    So flowing in its measure
    Is the rife cup of our pleasure,
As when with wand and pannier we tread the daisied valleys.

III.

Would we give the grey lark's carol for the cold lip-
uttered chorus,
>Or heaven's ample covering,
>Where the minstrel bird is hovering,

For the lamp-lit roofs that elevate their glimmering
arches o'er us?

IV.

Would we give our wild free rambles for the reveller's
heated prison?
>Or with the false and fawning
>Consume a summer's dawning,

Rather than greet the joyful sun from his couch of
clouds arisen?

V.

Would we give our water-sceptre for the staves of state
and splendour,
>Or exchange the angler's calling,
>On the shady river trolling,

For all the lesser pleasaunces that pomp or power can
tender?

VI.

Though bewitching are the hues that warp the world's
 every folly,
>   No longer they invite us,
>   While truer joys delight us
By the stream-side as we roam, below the hawthorn
 and the holly.

THE BONNIE TWEED.

I.

LET ither anglers chuse their ain,
    An' ither waters tak' the lead;
O' Hielan' streams we covet nane,
    But gie to us the bonnie Tweed!
An' gie to us the cheerfu' burn
    That steals into its valley fair—
The streamlets that at ilka turn
    Sae saftly meet an' mingle there.

II.

The lanesome Tala and the Lyne,
    An' Manor wi' its mountain rills,
An' Etterick, whose waters twine
    Wi' Yarrow frae the forest hills;

An' Gala, too, an' Teviot bright,
    An' mony a stream o' playfu' speed ;
Their kindred valleys a' unite
    Amang the braes o' bonnie Tweed.

III.

There's no a hole abune the Crook,
    Nor stane nor gentle swirl aneath,
Nor drumlie rill nor faery brook,
    That daunders thro' the flowery heath,
But ye may fin' a subtle troot,
    A' gleamin' ower wi' starn an' bead,
An' mony a sawmon sooms about
    Below the bields o' bonnie Tweed.

IV.

Frae Holylee to Clovenford,
    A chancier bit ye canna hae ;
So gin ye tak' an angler's word,
    Ye'd through the whuns an' ower the brae,

An' work awa wi' cunnin' hand
   Yer birzy hackles, black and reid ;
The saft sough o' a slender wand
   Is meetest music for the Tweed !
      Oh the Tweed ! the bonnie Tweed !
         O' rivers it's the best ;
      Angle here, or angle there,
      Troots are soomin' ilka where,
         Angle east or west.

THE BREEZE IS ON.

I.

The breeze is on the Heron Lake,
   The May-sun shineth clear;
Away we bound through the broomy brake,
   With our wands and angling gear.

II.

The birch-wreath o'er the water-edge
   Scatters sweet flies about,
And round his haunt of sighing sedge
   Bells up the yellow trout.

III.

Beware! beware! his eye is bright
   As falcon's in the sky;
But artful feather hove aright
   Will hood a keener eye.

IV.

Beware! beware the water-weed,
    And the birch that waves behind,
And gently let the good line speed
    Before thee on the wind.

V.

Oh! gently let the good line flow,
    And gently wile it home;
There's many a gallant fin, I trow,
    Under the ribbed foam.

VI.

A merry fish on a stallion hair
    'Tis a pleasant thing to lead
On May-days, when the cowslip fair
    Is blooming on the mead.

VII.

When the breeze is up, and the sun is out,
    And grey flies two or three

Sport in the noontide, round about
   The shadow of a tree.

VIII.

Oh! then the heart bounds pleasantly,
   And its thoughts are pleasant things,
Gushing in joyous purity,
   Like silent water-springs!

THE ANGLER'S INVITATION.

I.

Come when the leaf comes, angle with me,
Come when the bee hums over the lea,
    Come with the wild flowers—
    Come with the mild showers—
Come when the singing bird calleth for thee!

II.

Then to the stream side, gladly we'll hie,
Where the grey trout glide silently by,
    Or in some still place
    Over the hill face
Hurrying onward, drop the light fly.

III.

Then, when the dew falls, homeward we'll speed
To our own loved walls down on the mead,
    There, by the bright hearth,
    Holding our night mirth,
We'll drink to sweet friendship in need and in deed.

I SIT BY THE RIVER.

I.

I sit by the river and weep a farewell;
   My musings have turned to regrets,
While I gaze on the tranquil stream leaving the dell
   And the fisherman shooting his nets.

II.

Then rush to the memory summers of joy,
   And the shadowy sands of the past
Discover the wandering tracks of the boy
   Uninjured by billow or blast.

III.

Ah! each feat and each frolic, the pastimes of old,
   They seem as if left for me yet,
While afar on the indolent pool I behold
   The fisherman shooting his net.

IV.

But see! 'tis the silvery salmon that springs
    In mockery under the shade,
Below me the dark trout is rearing its rings,
    Unfettered and unafraid.

V.

Why grasp at the wand? what matters it now
    That they range unalarmed to my feet?
And alway, as the summer fly drops from the bough,
    Their wandering circles repeat?

VI.

Despoiled of the sorrowless scenes of my youth,
    I may toil my past loves to forget,
But Mem'ry will keep, 'mid her portraits of truth,
    The fisherman shooting his net.

THE ANGLER'S CHOICE.

THE ANGLER'S CHOICE.

I.

Where torrents foam,
While others roam
Among the yielding heather,
Some river meek
We'll forth and seek,
And lay our lines together.

II.

Some sylvan stream,
Where shade and gleam
Are blended with each other;
Below whose bank
The lilies lank
All humbler flowers ensmother.

III.

Where cushats coo
  And ring-doves woo
The shining channel over,
  From leafy larch
  Or birchen arch—
Their unmolested cover.

IV.

There daily met,
  No dark regret
Shall cloud our noon of pleasure;
  We'll carry rule
  O'er stream and pool
And none to claim a measure!

V.

With tackles rare
  On chosen hair,
March fly and minnow tender

We shall invite
The scaly wight
To eye them and surrender.

VI.

And when out-worn,
We'll seek some thorn
With shadow old and ample,—
The natural ground
Moss-laid around,
An angler's resting temple!

TO THE TWEED.

I.

Twined with my boyhood, wreathed on the dream
Of early endearments, beautiful stream!
The lisp of thy waters is music to me,
    Hours buried, are buried in thee!

II.

Sleepless and sinless, the mirth of thy springs!
The light, and the limpid—the fanciful things,
That mingle with thine the gleam of their play,
    And are lifted in quiet away!

III.

River! that toyest under the trees,
And lurest the leaf from the wandering breeze,
It glides over thee, like the gift of the young,
    When he rock'd at the bough where it hung

IV.

The voice of the city, the whisper of men,
I hear them, and hate them, and weary again
For the lull of the streams—the breath of the brae,
    Brought down in a morning of May.

V.

Go! hushed o'er thy channels, the shadow'd, the dim,
Give wail for the Stricken and worship to him,
That woke the old feats of the outlaw'd and free—
    The legends, that skirted on thee.

VI.

Broken the shell; but its lingering tone
Lives for the stream of his fathers—his own;
And the pale wizard hand, that hath gleaned out of eld.
    Is again on thy bosom beheld.

VII.

He hears not, but pilgrims that muse at his urn,
At the wailing of waters all tearfully turn.

And mingle their mourning, their worship in thine,
    And gather the dews from his shrine.

VIII.

Tweed! winding and wild! where the heart is unbound,
They know not, they dream not, who linger around,
How the sadden'd will smile, and the wasted re-win
    From thee—the bliss withered within.

IX.

And I, when to breathe is a burden, and joy
Forgets me, and life is no longer the boy,
On the labouring staff, and the tremorous knee,
    Will wander, bright river, to thee!

X.

Thoughts will come back that were with me before!
Loves of my childhood left in the core,
That were hushed, but not buried—the treasured—the true,
    In memory waken anew.

XI.

And the hymn of the furze, when the dew-pearls are shed,
And the old sacred tones of thy musical bed,
Will close, as the last mortal moments depart,
  The golden gates of the heart!

THE PIKE.

I.

GAILY rock the lily beds
   On the marge of Lomond lake;
There the lonely angler treads
   Nature round him—all awake,
      Heathy mountain
      And sweet fountain
   Stealing through the ferny brake.

II.

Swiftly from the water edge
   Shoots the fierce pike wing'd with fear,
To its lair among the sedge,
   As the angler wanders near,
      All elated,
      Primely baited,
   Seeking solitary cheer.

III.

Throbs aloud the eager heart
    And the hand in tremor moves,
When some sly fish all alert
    Round his tempting tackle roves.
        Boldly daring,
        Or bewaring,
    While the gleamy lure it proves.

IV.

Then at length, each doubt subdued
    Turns the lake-shark on his prey;
Quickly gorged the fatal food,
    Suddenly he darts away,
        All enshackled,
        Trimly tackled,
    Out into the deep'ning bay.

V.

But with steady caution schooled,
    Soon his wonted vigour fails.

By the angler's sceptre ruled
   Maimed the sullen pirate sails,
      Shoreward wending,
      Uncontending,
   Him the joyous captor hails.

VI.

And along the margin hauled,
   All his fretful fins aspread,
Tho' by subtle iron galled,
   Still he rears his gasping head
      Uncomplaining,
      Fear disdaining—
See him as a trophy led!

SONNET.

Of all sweet waters and soul-stirring spots,
Remote from the contentions of mankind,
Oftest repictured by my musing thoughts,
Lies a bright lake among fair trees enshrined,
Yclept Loch Achilty. A heath-grown crest
Surnamed the Tor its eastern guardian seems,
While wild Craig Darroch rears its hill of dreams
Emprisoning the clear wave on the west.
Bright mimic bays with weeping birches fringed—
An islet ruin—solitary deer—
And distant mountains by the sun-ray tinged
At the Mind's animating beck appear,
Nor un-remembered in the wizard scene,
Against a moss-grown stone, entranced two anglers lean.

THE HAPPY ANGLER.

I.

Below a shady hazel tree
    An angler trimmed his flies,
Singing, hey derry! trout that are merry
    No longer, no longer are wise.

II.

Of dapper make and ruddy hue
    'Twas a jolly blade, I ween,
With his hey derry, fresh from the ferry,
    Over the meadow so green.

III.

Right gladsomely he eyed the stream,
    And shook his wand anon,
With a hey derry! brown as a berry
    The winding waters run.

IV.

Oh! well I wot that jovial blade
   Is one of our gentle band,
With his hey derry, trout that are merry
   Swim to the angler's hand.
      Derry, hey derry!
      Trout that are merry
Swim to the angler's hand!

SONNET.

A METEOR-bearing bark before me made
For Tweed's wide current from a wooded bay
And under midnight's cover, on its way
Cautiously glided.   In its moving shade,
On either side the oar's infrequent blade
Dipped flagging, like the heron's wing—pursued
At every touch by fiery snakes, that play'd
Around the vessel's track.   A figure stood
Upon the prow with tall and threat'ning spear,
Which suddenly into the stream he smote.
Methought of Charon and his gloomy boat—
Of the torch'd Furies and of Pluto drear
Burning the Stygian tide for lamprey vile,
That on his bride's dimm'd face, Hell might behold a
    smile.

THE STREAMS OF OLD SCOTLAND.

I.

THE streams of old Scotland for me!
   The joyous, the wilful, the wild,
The waters of song and of glee,
That ramble away to the sea
   With the step and the mirth of a child!

II.

The valleys of England are wide;
   Her rivers rejoice every one,
In grace and in beauty they glide,
And water flowers float at their side,
   As they gleam in the rays of the sun.

III.

But where are the speed and the spray—
   The dark lakes that welter them forth—

Tree and heath nodding over their way—
The rock and the precipice grey,
   That bind the wild streams of the north?

IV.

Hath the salmon a dormient home
   In track of the barbel or bream?
Or holds he his fastness of foam,
Where the wraiths of the dark tempest roam
   At the break of a wandering stream?

V.

Even there you will find him, among
   The glens of old Scotland afar,
And up through her valleys of song,
He silently glances along
   In corselet of silver and star.

VI.

The rivers of Scotland for me!
   They water the soil of my birth,
They gush from the hills of the free
And sing, as they seek the wild sea,
   With a hundred sweet voices of mirth!

MY AIN WEE FISHER BOY.

I.

I lo'e my ain wee fisher boy,
   He's bold an' bonny—bonny an' bold,
An' aye there is a glint o' joy
   A-lyin' 'mang his locks o' gold.

II.

His gaud is o' the rowan rare ;
   It's braw an' bonny—bonny an' braw ;
His creel is o' the saugh sae fair
   That flowers below the castil wa'.

III.

I lo'e him for his sunny e'e.
   Sae blue an' sunny—sunny an' blue ;
There's glitterin' starns 'neath mony a bree
   But nane sae tender or sae true.

IV.

I lo'e him for his gentle airt,
   Wi' line an' angle—angle an' line,
He's captive ta'en my silly heart,
   This bonny fisher boy o' mine !

GOOD CHEER! BROTHER ANGLER.

I.

Good cheer! brother angler, say,
Is the swift salmon abroad to-day?
Have you noted the flash of his silv'ry mail,
Or the proud free curl of his glitt'ring tail?
Hath he sprung at the winsome fly,
    Smitten by the treacherous feather,
    Heedless of the steel and tether
And of human subtlety?

II.

Alas! brother angler, nay!
Salmon none have I stirred to-day—
Feint, frolic nor dart have I beheld,
But round me the wily dark trout bell'd;
One in greed and one in scorn,
    And a third one out of pleasure
    Sprang at my fly. See all the treasure
Ta'en by me this livelong morn!

III.

Ply on, brother angler! hark!
The grey wind warbles across the park;
It ruffles the water from bank to bank,
And shakes the green covert of rushes lank.
See how it paces round and round,
    Wild of foot—with step unsteady,
    Dancing on the amorous eddy
To a low, uncertain sound!

IV.

Ply on, brother angler! deep
Under the rapids the bright fins sweep,
And the salmon holdeth his secret track
O'er ledges of rock, through fissure black.
Oh! most hath an angler need
    Of sweet patience and of plodding;
    For the good wand ever nodding
Better than cunning bringeth speed!

A LOCH SCENE.

I.

A MOUNTAIN shadow lieth on
    Its mirror dark and massy;
The red late sun-ray streams across
O'er solemn wood and quiet moss,
    O'er sward and hillock grassy.

II.

It tinges with a crimson light
    The water sleeping under;
That calm clear water seldom wakes—
Calm when the forest pine-tree quakes—
    Calm 'mid the very thunder.

III.

A ruin on its islet stands,
    The walls with ivy pendent;
Its grey stones crumbling underneath
Peer through the arbitrary wreath
    Of that untrain'd ascendant.

IV.

But glancing from the record rude
    Of the remoter ages,
Behold the image of a stag
Timorous of the water flag
    Its eager thirst assuages!

V.

The stately antlers branching free
    Above its forehead tragic—
The form of animated grace
Are kindred to the quiet place,
    A portion of its magic!

VI.

And there the wild duck, like a skiff,
    Shoots from the reeds horrescent;
Its yellow paddles in their wake
Leave on the solitary lake
    The traces of a crescent.

VII.

The peerly water-heron, too,
　　Where the faint sun-ray trembles,
Drooping its ever graceful head
Above the floating lily-bed,
　　A poet-bird resembles.

VIII.

And yonder, on the distant marge,
　　Behold an angler eager,
With taper wand and arm of skill
Under the shadow of a hill—
　　A solitary figure.

IX.

But falling from the quiet air
　　The mist and shades together,
Glideth away the sad sweet show,
The mountain and the lake below—
　　The forest and the heather!

X.

And night with dewy forehead bent
    Holdeth her vigil solemn,
Till the red architect of morn
Upon a cloud-car slowly borne
    Erects his amber column.

OWER AT THE CAULD-FOOT.

I.

Ower at the cauld-foot
There bides an auld troot,
No mony there be that are wiser;
It baffles a' skill
To tether his gill
An' gie the sly boy a surpriser.

II.

He's thick an' he's braid
Wi' sprecks like a taed
An' spangles o' ilka dimension,
Mirk spangles an' reid
Frae his wacm to his heid,
In number ayont comprehension.

III.

Sic a swasher I ween
Is rare to be seen,
An' no to be grippit wi' thinkin;

It gars ilka chiel
Lay his loof on his reel
An' sets e'en the wisest a-blinkin'.

IV.

Auld Purdie cam' doon
Ane braw afternoon,
(Ilk angler taks choice o' his weather,)
Quoth he, "I'll soon bring
The knave to the spring
An' teach him the taste o' a feather."

V.

Sae e'en he set till't,
Like ane muckle skill't,
But faith, let the braggin' come last o't;
Frae the mirk till the dawin',
In spite o' his crawin',
He ne'er could mak oot the richt cast o't.

ANGLING SONGS.

VI.

There was Foster an' Kerse
An' a chiel frae the Merse
Wad set a' the water a seethin';
Watty Grieve an' Jock Hay
Cam ower the way
Wi' Scougal o' fair Innerleithen.

VII.

The mair were the han's,
The rifer the wan's,
Our king o' the cauld got the braver;
He bobbit aboot
Wi' his wonnerfu' snoot
An' cock't up his tail oot o' favour.

VIII.

But fling as they micht,
To the left or the richt,
Wi' mennin, mawk, lob, leech or rawin;

No a rug wad he gie,
For weel ettled he
his gear whilk the wind was a-blawin'.

IX.

Come, anglers, come a',
Baith meikle an' sma',
Tak yer chance o' the cunnin' auld reiver;
For aught that ye ken,
Mither Fortune may len'
Gude speed to yer wan's an' ye deive her.

THE ANGLER'S GRAVE.

I.

Sorrow, sorrow, bring it green!
  True tears make the grass to grow;
And the grief of the good, I ween,
  Is grateful to him that sleeps below.
Strew sweet flowers, free of blight—
  Blossoms gathered in the dew:
Should they wither before night,
  Flowers and blossoms bring anew.

II.

Sorrow, sorrow, speed away
  To our angler's quiet mound,
With the old pilgrim, twilight grey,
  Enter thou on the holy ground;

There he sleeps, whose heart was twined
    With wild stream and wandering burn,
Wooer of the western wind!
    Watcher of the April morn!

III.

Sorrow at the poor man's hearth!
    Sorrow in the hall of pride!
Honour waits at the grave of worth
    And high and low stand side by side.
Brother angler! slumber on,
    Haply thou shalt wave the wand,
When the tide of time is gone,
    In some far and happy land.

DRINKING SONG.

I.

DEATH, death to the bald-heads—no quarter!
    The rogues they shall taste of our steel;
We'll give each a turn of the torture,
    And lay him agape in the creel.

II.

Drink death to the bald-heads! why spare them?
    What matters it when they expire?
To say nay to our wishes we dare them,
    So re-strengthen the goblet still higher!

III.

Our wands to good fortune they guide us,
    Meanwhile, bear the cup to the mouth;
Let the break of grey twilight decide us
    And winds wand'ring soft from the south.

IV.

We anglers should quaff and be jolly,
 Ere the time to be doing draws nigh;
Short season will sleep away folly,
 And we'll up with the sun, by and by.

V.

Drink death to the bald-heads—no quarter!
 Why spare the sly rogues of the brook?
We'll give each a turn of the torture,
 Drink success to the wand and the hook!

THE FAIRY ANGLER.

I.

'Twas a bland summer's eve, when the forest I trod;
The dew-gems were starring the flowers of the sod,
And "faire mistress moone," as she rose from the sea,
Shed apart the green leaves of each shadowy tree.

II.

I passed by a brook, where her silvers lay flung,
Among knolls of wild fern it witchingly sung,
While a lone fairy angler with glimmering hand
From the odorous banks waved her delicate wand.

III.

In silence I watched, as with eager intent
O'er the moon-silvered water she gracefully bent,
And plied with green rush-rod, new torn from its bed,
Her line of the thorn-spider's mystical thread.

IV.

A pannier of moss-leaves her shoulders bedecked,
The nest of some bird, which the night winds had wrecked,
Slung round with a tendril of ivy so gay,
And a belt of stream flowers bound her woodland array.

V.

No snow-flake e'er dropt from its cloud on the brook
So gently impelled as her moth-plumaged hook;
The pearl-sided parlet and minnow obeyed
The magical beck of that wandering maid.

VI.

And aye as her rush-rod she waved o'er the rill,
Sweet words floated round her, I treasure them still,
Tho' like a bright moon-cloud resolved into air,
Passed from me, regretted, the vision so faire.

FAIRY'S SONG.

I.

No zephyr shakes the leafy, leafy tree;
   The round merry moon looks in on me,
     Through the grene-wood cover,
     Where all summer-night over,
My angle and I bear companye.

II.

I have haunts by the lone hill-cairn,
   There I trip it the frost-time thorough,
'Mong wild moss and faded fern,
   Where the blind mole rears his furrow;
I have haunts by the shell-strewn tide,
But better to me the sweet stream side,
     There the summer-night over,
     'Neath grene-wood cover
   My angle and I bear companye!

ANGLING ON A SUMMER NIGHT.

I.

Angling on a summer night,
    When the moon-ray met the fairy
Tripping down a bank of light,
    To the sweet loch of St. Mary;
Music floated sad and holy,
    Every wild flower lent its tone,
And the sullen trout swam slowly,
    Like the shadow of a stone.

II.

From the bank on Meggat stream,
    Where a quiet fountain gushes
And the undulating gleam
    Glances through a tuft of rushes;

There I threw the silv'ry palmer
    With a meditating arm,
For the crystal pool lay calmer
    Than a sea beneath a charm.

III.

Was it but a fancied fin
    O'er the glassy water gliding,
As I dropt the feather in,
    Like an insect half confiding,
Gently mov'd and lightly shaken—
    Neared a little—wiling out,
Till the fatal hook was taken
    By a huge and gleamy trout?

IV.

Quick as thought, the line unwound
    Flew along the streamlet narrow,
With the sharp and rapid sound
    Of a solitary arrow;

But a gentle effort leading
   On the bank the captive lay,
Tir'd, and quivering and bleeding,
   In his starry, rich array.

v.

Proudly gazed I to the lake,
   And the moonshafts, slant and slender,
On its bosom lay awake,
   Like an armoury of splendour;
Proudly gazed I to the mountain;
   Voices floated far and wide,
From the breeze, the flow'r, the fountain,
   Blessing me on every side!

ANGLING SONGS.

WE PART NOT THUS.

I.

We part not thus! nay, anglers, nay—
  A farewell to the season!
So fill the bowl and drink away;
  Who drinks not harbours treason.

II.

Oh fill it high! the joyous draught
  Is native to our heather;
If bravely drain'd and largely quaff'd,
  'Twill bind our hearts together.

III.

Now wintry winds with rapid pace
  O'er mead and mountain sally;
And gloomily the waters race
  Through each deserted valley.

IV.

No more, sweet birds, in merry strain,
    Sing from their bowers of beauty;
Lay down the wand—the spring again
    Will call it forth for duty.

V.

Lay down the wand—no longer now
    The fearful trout is belling;
All leafless left, the alder bough
    Moans o'er his glassy dwelling.

VI.

Then heap, heap high our social hearth!
    Why should the good fire flicker?
And quaff! quaff on! the best of mirth
    Lies deepest in the liquor!

ANGLING SONGS.

THE BURNING OF THE WATER.

I.

FLASHES the blood-red gleam
   Over the midnight slaughter;
Wild shadows haunt the stream,
   Dark forms glance o'er the water;
It is the leisterers' cry—
   A salmon, ho! oho!
In scales of light, the creature bright
   Is glimmering below.

II.

Murmurs the low cascade,
   The tall trees stand so saintly,
Under their quiet shade
   The river whispers faintly;
It is the leisterers' cry—
   The salmon, ho! oho!
A shining path the water hath
   Behind the shape of snow.

III.

Glances the ready spear
    From harmless hands unheeded,
On in its swift career
    The dream-like fish hath speeded;
It is the leisterers' cry—
    The salmon, ho! oho!
Along its wake, the torches break
    And waver to and fro.

IV.

Wildly the eager band
    Closes its fatal numbers;
Across its glistering sand
    The wizard water slumbers:
It is the leisterers' cry—
    The salmon, ho! oho!
And, lightning-like, the white prongs strike
    The jaded fish below.

V.

Rises the cheering shout
　　Over the rapid slaughter;
The gleaming torches flout
　　The old, oak-shadowed water.
It is the leisterers' cry—
　　The salmon, ho! oho!
Calmly it lies, and gasps, and dies
　　Upon the moss-bank low

THE LYNNS OF GLENDEVON.

I.

O'er the lynns of Glendevon, the dark trees hang crowded,
  While unseen whirl the waters below;
'Mid spray and thick foliage an angler enshrouded
  Waves his wand—waves his wand to and fro.

II.

In the lynns of Glendevon, from deep crevice stealing,
  The hungry trout watches its prey,
And when 'mid the white foam some stray fly lies wheeling,
  Slyly bears—slyly bears it away.

III.

Alas! among morsels the sweetest and rarest,
  That float down the streams of the brake,
Deceits ever mingle, in colours the fairest,
  Capturing those—capturing those who partake.

IV.

'Tis thus in this bright world, at joys without measure
    Unheeding we ardently spring,
And forget that oft hid by the plumage of pleasure,
    Lies a hook—lies a hook in the wing.

SONNET—THE FINDHORN.

To the monastic mind thy quiet shade
Kindly accords, bewild'ring Darnaway!
Here, those retiring Powers, whose hermit sway
The hordes of gross emotions hold obey'd
Reign indolent, on bank or flow'ry glade.
A deep unusual murmur meets my ear,
As if the oak's Briarean arms were sway'd
Far off in the weird wind.   Like timorous deer
Caught as he browses by the hunter's horn,
I stop perplex'd, half dreading the career
Of coming whirlwind.   Then with conquer'd fear
Advancing softly through a screen of thorn,
From edge of horrid rock, abruptly bold,
Rushing thro' conduit vast, swart Findhorn I behold.

FISHER WATTY.

I.

Fisher Watty's dead an' gane,
  Death amang his cairns has gripp't him;
Aft afore, whan he wad fain
Hae made the kittle chiel his ain,
  Watty gied a flaff an' slipt him.

II.

Noo at length the mools amang,
  The elrich carle has laid him fairly;
Quoth he, "Ye've play'd yer pliskies lang,
My faith! but ye maun end yer sang
  An' pack awa to saxton Charlie."

III.

Waes me! sin' canny Wat's awa,
  I feel sae lanesome an' sae weary,

Tho' simmer winds abune me blaw,
Ilk burnie seems a rin o' snaw
   An' Tweed gangs daundrin', douf an' dreary.

IV.

Aft I clim' the bosky brae,
   Aft I seek the haly rowan,
At the gloamin' o' the day,
Ere the starns begin their sway—
   Whan the lav'rock woos the gowan.

V.

Aft I wanner to the stane
   The warlock stane whar late we parted :
Waes me ! sin' Fisher Watty's gane,
My souple wan' I wald alane,
   Wi' feckless arm, ower pools deserted.

VI.

Here, the hazel boughs aboon,
   That to their mirror beck sae gaily,

Puir Wat upon an April noon
Gied his last fish its deadly stoun',
   An' as it wambled, gaff'd it brawly.

VII.

There, in yonner stream sae blate,
   Quoth he, "Whane'er the cock's a-crawin',
Anither cast we'll aiblins get;"
But death was tirlin' at his yett
   An hour or twa afore the dawin'.

VIII.

In the kirk-yaird beild sae green,
   Auld Watty's laid by saxton Charlie,
An' ay on ilka simmer's e'en
I think upon the time that's been—
   An' as I wanner, miss him sairly.

www.ingramcontent.com/pod-product-compliance
Lightning Source LLC
Chambersburg PA
CBHW021205230426
43667CB00006B/562